Trying Cases: Promise, Prove, and Persuade

TRYING CASES: PROMISE, PROVE, AND PERSUADE
A manual for law students and young lawyers

JENNIFER ZEDALIS

This book is dedicated to my Husband, Timothy,
whose love and support makes all things possible in my life.

TRYING CASES: PROMISE, PROVE, AND PERSUADE
A manual for law students and young lawyers

Jennifer Zedalis

Published by:

Vandeplas Publishing, LLC – July 2018

801 International Parkway, 5th Floor
Lake Mary, FL. 32746
USA

www.vandeplaspublishing.com

ISBN 978-1-60042-276-8

To an observer, a lawyer's role in the courtroom may appear deceptively easy. A well-prepared lawyer is easy to understand and helpful to jurors. The backstory of all good trial lawyers is rich with experience, spirit, courage, and empathy. Layers of thought and effort make up the final product a lawyer brings to court. Great lawyers speak to jurors in a way that makes their cases not only compelling but irresistible.

Any case can be presented with courage and preparation. Some cases are very challenging, and others are easier. Clients sometimes go to trial because they have a strong case. Others end up in trial because simpler methods of dispute resolution have failed. Despite profound advances in technology, resourceful uses of data, and a broad array of dispute resolution methods, lawyers still find themselves in front of jurors. Clients still need brilliant lawyers in the courtroom.

Think for a moment about the bill of rights. Think about liberty and its twin, freedom. Think about security, privacy, and property rights. Whenever a lawyer stands before a jury in this country, rights and interests are at stake. Some involve criminal justice and others involve civil protections. Because people value safety, privacy, property, and liberty, the right to trial remains precious.

For a client facing trial, a good lawyer is essential. Trial advocacy makes the constitutional right to a fair trial meaningful. Without the dedication and skill of a good lawyer, a fair trial would be difficult or impossible to realize.

Trials engage lawyers in a complex group of demanding tasks. Many things are happening at once. At a given point in trial, a lawyer might need to control an adverse witness, protect a client, persuade the jurors, and make a record for appeal.

Lawyers must listen carefully to what is happening during trial. It is unwise or even dangerous to sit at counsel table studying a pretrial script. Although preparation is essential, trial lawyers must understand how to do their job from moment to moment. Whenever a witness adds a new element to the story or an opposing lawyer tries an unexpected tactic, a trial lawyer must be prepared to act or adjust accordingly. In trial, lawyers must make decisions and judgement calls every few minutes. They must be ready to adapt, revise, recall, and overcome. They must listen with the ears of a juror, think like a witness, and speak to a potential appeals court at the same time. Sometimes the most difficult task is to find a way of presenting the case that is compatible with all these needs.

Lawyers must understand the rules of evidence and their application to the facts of the case. To handle motions and objections intelligently, lawyers must understand the unique relation of one fact in a case to the other facts. They must know the facts well enough to relate them to claims, defenses, and credibility. They must also understand how to lay foundations for expert testimony and non-testimonial evidence.

Facts are like tangible things in the trial process– they have colors, texture, shape, and size. Lawyers must come to know the facts dearly as they work the case into trial posture. They must discover the facts and "wear" them long before the trial to see how they fit. As lawyers conduct fact investigation and participate in discovery, cases begin to take on personality and character. Some cases are simpler than others. All cases are important.

The goal of this book is to energize and inspire young lawyers with a template for courtroom success. The value of trial skills should not be underestimated. Trials are profoundly important in the lives and fortunes of those who find themselves in a lawsuit. When called upon to present a client's case to a jury, a lawyer should be prepared, skilled, and genuine.

Although lawyers must work with what they find during discovery, they have enormous influence on the way jurors *feel* about cases. Lawyers must deal with the big picture, the bottom line, and the small details. How does a good lawyer get started?

TABLE OF CONTENTS

PREPARING FOR TRIAL

Every chapter of this book has an underlying presumption of preparedness. The ideas and examples will be unhelpful to lawyers who fail to investigate their cases and exhaust all avenues of discovery. The hard work begins well before the eve of trial. The facts must be known and understood in detail before critical decisions are made. Cases must be developed based on what happened and who can come to court and testify about it. Lawyers should not stop investigating and gathering information until they have a full picture and a rich sense of how a case will look and sound in court.

What are the claims or charges in the case? What are the defenses? What laws apply? What is the burden, and who has it? What is the human story in the case? Who will testify, and what will they say? What is the background of the people in the story? How are jurors likely to react to the people, the visual evidence, and the issues in the trial?

Are there motions that should be argued before trial? Are there concerns about admissibility of evidence? Has all the necessary research been done? How will the verdict form be structured?

There will always be surprises. Witnesses will forget. Some will deliberately change their story. Some will move away or pass away. The opposing party will sometimes change strategy, abandon a claim or argument, or focus on something unexpected. A new judge may be assigned to the case before the trial date. Judges sometimes rule in unexpected ways on pretrial motions. Because trials never play out exactly like the investigative or discovery phases, lawyers must know the case very well. Critical last-minute decisions will need to be made during every trial.

Good lawyers keep working on a case until they have come *full-circle* in both factual and legal investigation. In other words, they keep reading, visiting, interviewing, questioning, researching, studying, developing potential strategies, and considering various approaches until they continually arrive at the same place.

If questions remain that are possible to answer, they find the answers. If there are variables in the case, the risks and unknowns are factored into preparation.

Valuable insights are gained whenever a lawyer looks at the case from the viewpoint of the opponent. Where is the client's case most vulnerable? What are the strengths for the other side? In all cases, there are hard and soft facts. Hard facts are facts that are not in dispute. Soft facts are facts that will be contested. Some positions are risky. Others are safer. The facts of a case are like a landscape. Lawyers must find the best paths through these areas and determine the best landing position for the client.

Trial preparation should never be rigid. Good trial lawyers are flexible. No matter how well they prepare, everything they bring with them into the courtroom is conditional. In most cases, lawyers spend more time *listening* in trial than they do talking. They don't want to miss a thing the jury is hearing or seeing, whether it is favorable or harmful. They must be able to adjust as the case unfolds.

SAMPLE CHECK LIST FOR TRIAL.

> Pleadings (all parties)
> Jury Instructions (standard instructions and proposed special instructions)
> Proposed verdict form
> Witness List
> Exhibits List
> Pretrial Orders (including rulings on pretrial motions)
> Order of proof for case-in-chief
> Witness Files (discovery pertaining to each witness; prep for direct or cross; subpoena information)
> Rules and Case Law for anticipated motions and objections
> Outlines for jury selection
> Outlines for opening statement and closing argument
> Last minute to-do list

When a lawyer promises a strong case, jurors sit up and take notice. They wait. They listen. They want proof. Everyone in the courtroom knows the ultimate outcome of the trial is important-- perhaps critically so.

Trials impact the lives of many people. They have profound impact on the lives of litigants. Families and communities are impacted. Lawyers, witnesses, judges, and jurors remember trials for the rest of their lives. Verdicts have life changing consequences. Trials are memorable.

From the first moments in a trial, an unspoken truth hangs over the people assembled in the courtroom: All else has failed. Negotiations have been unsuccessful. There has been no meeting of the minds and no agreement between the parties. There is a contest. There are competing versions of the story. There is at least one party with a burden of proof. Jurors will now be called upon to hear the case and decide the verdict.

How does a young lawyer get to that place where the promise and the proof come together? What are the skills and tools of persuasion?

Hard work is the biggest force behind a great trial lawyer. Focused, sustained effort is a necessary part of a trial lawyer's day-to-day life. Lawyers learn by observing, listening, and doing. It is important to be reflective. Great trial lawyers have a high capacity for self-evaluation. They learn from experience. They also have these qualities:

BRAVERY.

Lawyers need reserves of courage. There will be difficult cases. There will be unpopular clients. There will be unpredictable witnesses. There will be adverse rulings. There will be disappointing verdicts.

INTELLECTUAL INDEPENDENCE.

Great lawyers are free from myths, marketing lore, and canned scripts. These are no substitute for knowing the case and everyone in it very well. Every case is unique. In each part of a trial, the goals must be tailored to suit the needs of the client.

HONESTY AND REALISM.

Some cases are won because of hard work, preparation, and skill. Other cases are won because one side had much better facts than the other. Whether the verdict is won or lost, good lawyers evaluate their own work with honesty and objectivity. Every trial is a learning experience.

EGO MANAGEMENT.

Be conscious of the needy ego. The case is about the client and not about the lawyer. Lawyers who carry a big ego into trial often become exhausted by the sheer weight of it. In the courtroom, lawyers need all their intellectual and emotional energy for their clients and the demands of justice, whatever those may be.

Command of the Courtroom

Capture and hold the jurors' attention.

Choose words that fit the case.

Find words in the case.

Practice word economy (less is more).

Use juror-friendly words.

Find themes in the case.

Be visual.

Be mindful of clues.

GOOD FACTS DON'T MATTER UNLESS THE JURORS ARE PAYING ATTENTION.

No matter how strong the case is, it will suffer with a weak courtroom advocate. If jurors are bored, they will miss the proof. Jurors lose interest or find it difficult to pay attention when a lawyer:

Reads a prepared script;
Uses legal or tedious language;
Talks too much;
Speaks in a monotone;
Speaks too loudly;

Mumbles;

Speaks too fast;

Hesitates too often;

Sends mixed signals;

Or acts as if much of what he is doing is guesswork.

As soon as possible, aspiring trial lawyers should become familiar and comfortable in the courtroom space. Lawyers interact with courtroom space much like actors in a theatre, except the events and consequences of courtroom cases are real. Lawyers must be interesting enough to hold the attention of their audience, the jury. They must be interesting without being distracting. They must be aware of their own voice, tone, and pace without being self-conscious. They must understand how to translate the case events into a persuasive courtroom story.

ADVOCACY CALLS FOR THOUGHTFUL WORD CHOICE.

Words and language have special value in trial, because that is where persuasion begins. To be persuasive, lawyers must be good communicators. Good communicators train just like athletes. They are discriminating in their choice of words and in what they choose to leave unspoken. Trial lawyers learn to appreciate the richness of language, including subtle differences in meaning, descriptive adjectives and adverbs, and local usage.

Good lawyers understand the importance of simplicity. They understand the principle of economy of language– less is often more. They think about tone and emphasis. They understand the importance of listening. Communication is not just an initiative-- it is also a responsive thing.

In trial, lawyers must divide their energy between speaking and listening.

Persuasion is an art. Experience, skills, habits, talents, gifts, and many unknowns figure into the mix that informs a lawyer's persuasive ability. A limited but important part of persuasive ability can be addressed in textbooks. Communication skills are essential to persuasion.

What are the qualities of great communicators? Why do jurors want to hear some lawyers and prefer to daydream when others are at the podium? Why do some lawyers command attention while others put jurors to sleep, or alienate everyone in the courtroom?

Good lawyers concentrate on words and language when preparing cases. They think about how the case will sound. They think about the best words and the most compelling themes in the case. The development of language skills begins so early that it is generally taken for granted by the time students enter law school. A lawyer should give conscious thought to *how* he tells his client's story. How should the events be described? How can the good parts be highlighted with spirit, and the bad parts lessened or neutralized with credibility and grace?

Communication depends on both preparedness and adaptability. Good trial lawyers think about what to say and how to say it as they develop their case for trial. They must also develop skill at thinking on their feet. Trial advocacy is very different from appellate advocacy. Things are happening moment to moment in trial. The record is being made moment to moment. The jurors are listening. Witnesses are testifying. There is no time to proof-read. Unless there is a mistrial or a successful appeal, there will be no do-over. Most often, the trial is a time of "now or never".

In trial, lawyers must hear everything jurors hear, process it, and decide how to deal with it in the context of the case. They must decide quickly. What needs to be emphasized? What are the best ways to help jurors understand the case in a way that is favorable to the client? How should the case be presented, explained, translated, or made more appealing?

Some words are very good for trial and others are less useful or even harmful. Trial words should be words which best fit the client's story. These are often the first words which come to mind when thinking about the case. What are the themes in the case? Is the case about jealousy? Fear? Greed? Carelessness? Mental illness? Are there key words or phrases which capture the action in the case? Will key witnesses use words or phrases which should be adopted by the lawyer? Which words will jurors readily understand and appreciate more than others?

Admissions and excited utterances are very powerful in the courtroom. In the heat of a moment, things get screamed, whispered, e-mailed, or texted which capture the proof necessary for a favorable verdict. Exact words are sometimes crucial for success. Jurors want to know more than the actions of key players. They want to know the thoughts and motivations. They want the truth, which is often surrounded by drama. The lawyer who makes a case richer by introducing these valuable words has an advantage.

The *way* lawyers say what they say is also important. Successful trial law-yers are very aware of their audience. They are not drafting a brief or writing a scholarly paper. They are in the moment, and their audience is the jury. They are genuine and sincere. They are not condescending or cryptic.

Consider public speaking– it is easy to tell when a politician or entertainer is speaking from a prepared script. The words are not delivered with spontaneity. Recitation isn't knowledge. When a speaker is reading, it is easy to come away with the feeling that the speaker doesn't *know* what he is talking about.

Canned speech is not persuasive. Someone who knows *nothing* about the case can stand up and read a speech. Persuasive lawyers speak directly to jurors. Persuasive lawyers *know what happened.* They speak to jurors with the sponta-neity and feeling of an eye witness. Without melodrama or contrived emotions, they capture the respect and interest of the jury.

When a lawyer addresses the jury, it should be apparent that she knows what happened in the case and what the issues are. She should choose simple, eloquent words. She should draw upon themes with universal meaning and appeal. Lawyers who over-dress a case with exaggeration or salesman pitches sacrifice credibility. Lawyers who clutter a case with jargon, excess words, or unfamiliar words put distance between the case and the jurors.

Every moment a juror loses trying to figure out what a lawyer is saying or what he *really* means is damaging to the client. Like everyone else, jurors have finite patience and finite attention spans. Good lawyers do the "word work" up front so the case is simple and meaningful for the jurors. Good lawyers also *listen carefully* throughout the trial, and make any necessary changes based on the way the case is coming across.

Sometimes lawyers find themselves dealing with cryptic language or "code". There may be unfamiliar terms used by key players in the story. Scientific and technical terms also come up. It's important to help jurors understand these terms and become familiar with them. This can often be done in opening state-ment. If necessary, jurors should get a clear, simple definition from a qualified witness. Jurors need to work through facts and issues without having to wonder or guess the meaning of unfamiliar terms.

Lawyers should adopt important words or phrases used by witnesses in the case. The repetition makes it easier for jurors to remember important details. Staying close to an eye witness's descriptive style is more genuine than laying lawyer talk on top of the case. Lawyers who are genuine are powerful.

It is also important to note the *precise* words used by opposing witnesses. It is easier to catch a witness in a lie or a memory lapse if he is confronted with his own words. Admissions are more powerful if they are unique to individuals. Quotes are powerful.

To avoid credibility problems, lawyers should select the most interesting and descriptive terms that *accurately* describe what happened. In other words, the promise should match the proof. Exaggeration leads to trouble when it's time for closing argument. Jurors will look and listen for proof. If the proof is well below the promise, it will be much like the boy who cried "Wolf!" too often.

Consider the difference between the following words, even though they might be used to describe the same condition:

injured; hurt; wounded; maimed; disabled; disfigured

worried; concerned; troubled; scared; alarmed; frightened; terrorized; frantic

mist; shower; rain; downpour; storm; drizzle; deluge

disgruntled; angry; irritated; enraged; ticked off; livid; peeved

embarrassed; ashamed; humiliated; red-faced; disrespected

Word choice should be based on the facts of the case, themes in the case, quotes of key witnesses, and jury appeal. Jurors are human beings. They do not operate like computers. They are not a form of artificial intelligence. Although verdicts should be based on the facts and the law, the way jurors *feel* about the story and the players will influence their decisions immeasurably.

A trial may be a story, a pair of stories, or a story told by different voices. The side that does the best job telling the story has a better chance of being persuasive. Jurors pay attention when they have an interesting case to follow.

Lawyers must take witnesses as they find them, but a word-conscious lawyer has any number of ways to paint a picture of the case when addressing the jury.

Some words evoke positive images, and some evoke negative images. In a thrift store, for example, one piece of furniture might be described in the following terms by different shoppers:

shabby-chic; vintage; used; second-hand; has character; fixer-upper; retro; nostalgic;

old; outdated; obsolete; antique; ancient; charming; Grandma's; worn out; run down

It is useful for lawyers to think of language in terms of **guilty words** and **innocent words,** or in civil cases, **liable words** and **not-liable words**, and so forth. A defense attorney should not refer to his own client as "the defendant". The word "defendant" is impersonal, and it also has negative or guilty connotations. There are many ways to express the same facts. Some favor the speaker's party, and some favor the opponent's. Jurors hear the differences and the nuances whether they are intended or accidental.

For good trial lawyers, nothing about word choice is accidental.

Consider these examples:

Now, **admittedly,** my client had been drinking with his buddies that evening.

My client attended a social event with school friends that evening, and they drank some beer.

Unfortunately, we **cannot deny** that my client was drinking that evening.

Which of the above sounds better for the client?

He **confessed** to what had happened that night.[1]

---

1   The term 'confession' suggests an admission of guilt and would therefore be a mis-characterization if used by a lawyer to describe a statement which is either exculpatory or neutral. For example, if an accused person says she shot someone but goes on to explain the shooting was an accident, it is a statement, but it is not an admission of guilt.

He *cooperated* with police, and he told them what happened that night.

He gave a *voluntary statement* about what happened that night.

Which of the above sounds most *innocent?*

Ms. Jones will tell you her *story* here today.

Ms. Jones will tell you *what happened* that night.

Which of the above is most persuasive?

Good lawyers are aware of word *culture.* Language develops as technology makes more forums available. New words and phrases come into use as generations of children become adults and expand their presence in social media and various fields of work. New phrases are "coined" every year.

Lawyers should make sure the language and terms they choose can be readily understood by all the jurors, including those who are not active in social media or otherwise drawn to popular culture. Some jurors might not understand a reference or phrase associated with a popular television program. Others might be unfamiliar with the refrain from a popular song. Jurors who are left out of the culture club may become frustrated or angry.

PRACTICE WORD ECONOMY: LAWYERS WHO CAN SAY THE *MOST* WITH THE *FEWEST WORDS* ARE THE EASIEST TO LISTEN TO.

Imagine you are listening to the case as a juror. More words mean more work for those who need to figure out what happened and how to decide the case. A good trial lawyer can do twice as much as a poor one in the same length of time by avoiding unnecessary words and understanding when repetition has become counter-productive. Editing should become a conscious part of trial preparation. Openings, closings, and questions suffering from word clutter make tedious work for the jurors. Editing becomes a conscious part of a good lawyer's courtroom speech pattern.

Economy in word choice is helpful throughout the entire trial. Lawyers who repeat too often and throw the kitchen sink into their cases come off as unprepared.

A strong theme is worth repeating. There are times when repetition is helpful. There are also limits. The lawyer's trained "juror's ear" should warn when a phrase is becoming sing-song. Good opening statements and closing arguments are fact-rich rather than repetitive. Powerful facts and themes can be emphasized with changes in tone, pauses, or silence. Powerful arguments should be backed up with facts, not repetition.

In jury selection, lawyers should ask simple, neutrally phrased questions. More words used by a lawyer in jury selection means less time for each potential juror to share experiences, attitudes, and views. Regardless of their ages or educational backgrounds, jurors appreciate simplicity. Simply-worded questions are an excellent resource during this important part of the process. Jurors can understand simple questions right away. They are less intimidated, and they feel more comfortable sharing information.

Word economy is also important for opening statements. Good lawyers edit their opening statements for the most impact and appeal. A well-opened case is one with highlights and key facts. What will capture the hearts, minds, and ears of the jurors? Can the client's story be told in simple, captivating terms? Are there smaller, less important details that can be edited from the opening? Will there be so much detail in the opening statement that the jurors grow weary trying to commit it to memory? Will there be unnecessary details that the witnesses may not even deliver during the trial? Will the opening be so wordy that it becomes confusing?

In closing argument, long, detailed recitations of the evidence tend to sound like transcripts. A lawyer should not sound like a court reporter. It is more effective to make compelling arguments punctuated with supporting facts. Photographs and tangible evidence can often do more than words. Lawyers should consider the impact of non-testimonial evidence when addressing the jury. At times, it is best to stop talking altogether in favour of a powerful picture or object.

Silence is an excellent resource for lawyers.

It is frustrating for jurors when a lawyer throws too many words into the case. In some instances, it is also poor grammar. Longer openings, longer questions, longer words, and longer arguments do not add up to a better verdict. Consider the following choice of phrases, and think about whether it is helpful or tedious to string words of like meaning together:

The strong force was very extreme.
The force was extreme. (best)

He had hidden secrets. (redundant)
He had secrets. (best)
He kept hidden secrets from other people. (redundant)
They both looked just alike. (redundant)
They were both identical. (redundant)
They were identical. (good)
They were alike. (best)
They both had the same identical look. (redundant)

She did an investigation of the circumstances surrounding the death. (too many words)
She looked at the circumstances that surrounded the death. (too many words)
She investigated the death. (best)

In the above examples, the shortest expression is the best one. The shortest example is also grammatically proper.

In addition to causing word clutter, extra words will sometimes alienate or distract jurors. Consider these potential phrases in the defense's opening. The case involves a death:

It was just an accident. (trivializes the death)
It was an accident. (describes an unintentional act without trivializing the death)

Lawyers who want to help the jury understand and follow the case will choose common, simple language. They will use words that people hear every day instead of technical jargon or words which are not part of generally spoken vocabulary. Poor advocates will use overly technical words and legal or law enforcement jargon.

Here are different ways of explaining what Officer Pop did in State v. Mop:

At approximately 0300 hours on the date of the incident, Law Enforcement Officer Pop proceeded to a single-family residence located at 1012 East 10th Street in Geesville, Aldo County, Florida. At that point and time, Officer Pop parked and proceeded to exit his marked patrol vehicle. Officer Pop then proceeded on foot to the front entrance of the residence and knocked on the door. There, he made contact with a female individual by the name of Jane Mop. Ms. Mop was then determined to be the owner of the residence at that location. (word clutter, law enforcement jargon)

On June 10th at about three in the morning, Officer Pop went to the house at 1012 East 10th Street in Geeville, where he met with the homeowner, Jane Mop. (simple and clear)

<u>Which of the above examples would be most helpful for jurors?</u>

THEMES SHOULD BE CAPTURED AND EXPRESSED IN THE LANGUAGE OF THE CASE.

Themes aren't *made* for cases– the theme of a case is *found* in the facts and issues. The facts dictate the theme. Themes are broader and more powerful than the underlying legal theory. Legal claims or charges are based upon theories of recovery, liability, excuse, guilt, or innocence. In contrast, themes pull the human dimension of the case into the jurors' decision-making process.

For example, legal theories include negligence, assumption of the risk, specific performance, lack of causation, necessity, self-defense, premeditation, and insufficient evidence. Theories are often formalized in statutes and jury instructions.

Themes are closer to the universal knowns of human behavior. Some common themes are greed, carelessness, recklessness, loyalty, lust, anger, vanity, control, jealousy, fear, illness, and dishonesty. A theme may be explicit or implicit, depending on the trial plan of the lawyer. The theme must be compatible with the theory of the case to further the interests of the client.

Here are some examples of the relationship between theory and theme: If the defense attorney's theory of the case is self-defense, then the theme might be "survival," or "kill or be killed." Another way of expressing the same theme might be "He had less than a second to choose. He chose to live." There may be a powerful quote from a party or witness that captures the theme of the case. Sometimes lawyers must look elsewhere to find a universally recognizable theme that works naturally in the case. Themes capture emotional and factual truths.

If the theory of recovery is that a company knowingly failed to warn of the risks associated with use of its product, the theme might be "profits over safety", or "they could have saved so many with so little".

There are often competing themes. For example, if the plaintiff's theme is greed, the defense may have a competing theme consistent with the issue of causation: blaming others for your own mistakes. If the prosecution's theme is greed or self-interest of the defendant, the defense might use the same theme in a different way, focusing on the self-serving interests of the government informant.

Themes are powerful resources for opening statements and closing arguments. They are like threads, running through the case and tying the facts together. Lawyers use themes to inform other decisions, like word choice, which evidence to emphasize, and how to structure witness examinations.

Themes give the jurors context in which to place people, events, and evidence. In some cases, there will be sub-themes or implicit themes as well.

BE VISUAL. CONSIDER SIGHT AS A COMPANION TO SOUND.
WHAT JURORS *SEE* IN THE COURTROOM IS AS IMPORTANT AS
WHAT THEY *HEAR*.

Visual aids are an excellent way of bringing a case to life. Like formally admitted exhibits, visual aids are an important trial resource for lawyers.

Examples of visual aids:

A timeline
A slide or large poster showing:
 the effects of a prescription drug over time
 the value of a certain stock over time
 different statements a witness has made over time
 the elements of a crime
 a jury instruction
 the elements of a civil rights violation

Whenever charts, diagrams, or slides are used, they should be easy to see and easy to understand. Complex, highly detailed exhibits are not as effective. Jurors get more from an exhibit when they can quickly understand and absorb the content.

CLUES ABOUT THE CASE ARE IMPORTANT.

On some level, jurors are aware of everything they see and hear in the courtroom. Jurors are influenced by *clues*. They are influenced consciously and unconsciously. Lawyers should be aware of everything that is going on in the courtroom when jurors are present. Facial expressions and tone of voice are noticed by jurors. They notice the way lawyers interact with clients and witnesses.

Jurors notice manner of dress, attitude, and speech. They scrutinize judges, lawyers, clients, and witnesses. They obtain clues about credibility, believability, and the confidence level of the lawyers by using all their senses. When a witness is giving highly damaging or emotional testimony, jurors will often look over at the other side to see how the opposing party is reacting.

REMEMBER THE AUDIENCE.

If the jurors could "change the channel" or get to a different "website" in the courtroom, would they do so? When would they prefer to replay or fast-forward? Would they prefer to turn the sound up, or off? Are they captivated, or has their attention wandered elsewhere?

JURY SELECTION

Who are these people?

How will their experiences and viewpoints influence the way they feel about the case?

How should cause and peremptory challenges be exercised?

Jury selection, or *voir dire*,[2] is a challenging process. It takes practice to become truly skilled at jury selection. The most seasoned trial lawyers must still prepare mentally for this stage of trial.

Jury selection sets the tone for the rest of the trial. It is the only time lawyers are permitted to ask jurors what they are thinking, and the only time lawyers are actively engaged in learning about the jurors. In other parts of the trial, lawyers are only able to guess what jurors are thinking by observing their reactions and their level of attention.

The courtroom is an uncomfortable place for strangers to talk to each other. In the formal and intimidating atmosphere of a courtroom, it is difficult for a lawyer to learn about the people who may end up deciding his client's fate or to help them understand jury service. Courtrooms are adversarial forums. In the minds of jurors, courtrooms are associated with catastrophic events, injury, bad acts, ill will, drama, and (hopefully) justice, but *not* enjoyment, small talk, or relaxation.

Many lawyers feel awkward about jury selection. They may feel as if they are under a microscope even though they are the ones asking the questions. They may feel uncomfortable asking people about their experiences and views.

Judges play a role in introducing jurors to the trial process, and they exercise control in the courtroom. Within that framework, lawyers also educate jurors

---

2   To speak the truth. Blacks Law Dictionary, p. 1746

about the process and, to some extent, the issues in the case. It is an exchange. Lawyers must learn enough about each potential juror to intelligently exercise cause and peremptory challenges. Jurors must learn enough about the process to get their role right.

It is best to adopt an all-out approach when learning how to select a jury. This chapter is focused on state court practice, as the role of lawyers in federal jury selection is usually more limited.

It is helpful to *observe* jury selection early and often. When law students and young lawyers observe jury selection, they can focus on the way lawyers ask questions and see how much useful information they get without having to worry about the result.

Observers should think critically about the process. How are the lawyers coming across? How much are the lawyers *learning* about the jurors? Are the jurors talking? Do they seem comfortable answering the lawyers' questions? Do the answers seem candid? Are the answers revealing? Are the jurors forthcoming? Do they volunteer information? Are they willing to share their views on sensitive topics?

Does the resulting jury seem like the best possible jury for the case? Which side did the best job? Does one side already have an advantage based on the selection?

It is not a good practice to re-invent the wheel or be too creative in jury selection. It is important to ask straightforward questions that allow jurors to talk about experiences and views relevant to the case. Lawyers should do everything possible to help jurors appreciate the need for candid and full disclosure during the process. They should think carefully about what to ask and how to ask it.

It is helpful to study the jury selection outlines of experienced lawyers and develop a feel for the territory. The type of case dictates the topics to be covered. There are no crystal balls, but it is usually possible to identify areas where personal experiences and biases of potential jurors need to be explored. Ironically, the larger part of jury selection is deciding who needs to be *excused,* not *selected.* Lawyers who draw attention to favorable jurors may end up helping their opponents more than their own clients. Both sides are continually thinking about how to exercise challenges.

Specific skills are needed to realize the goals of jury selection. Lawyers must be skillful at:

Phrasing questions in a neutral (non-threatening) way.

Getting jurors to feel comfortable.

Getting jurors to talk about their experiences.

Getting jurors to talk about their views/ beliefs.

Getting jurors to be candid.

Getting jurors to be truthful.

Getting jurors to understand their role.

Getting jurors to understand the honor system.

Educating jurors in a way that supports the client's position.

Jurors operate on an honor system. From the moment they take an oath to be truthful during jury selection to the moment they tell the judge their verdict is indeed their *true and lawful* verdict, they are on an honor system.

What should a lawyer say to jurors to get them thinking about the importance of the honor system?

Sample jury selection questions are available in law firm libraries, on line, and in trial advocacy resources. Some will be well-suited to the case being tried. Potential questions should be studied. Good questions should be adopted. Lawyers should never be tempted to adopt a jury selection outline just because other lawyers have used it or because it saves time. All questions should be phrased with juror-friendly words. It is a good idea to go over potential questions with colleagues. A well-prepared outline is just a starting point, but it is an important one.

Questions should be phrased in a way that is *neutral* enough to keep jurors comfortable and encourage candid answers. No one wants to volunteer information in a judgmental atmosphere. Jurors should be made to feel as if they are in a judgment-free zone. Everyone's views are respected in the zone. Everyone's experiences are important in the zone. Everyone is valued in the zone.

No one wants to be tested. Jurors don't want to feel as if the only people worthy of jury duty are the ones who can "pass" the lawyer's "test". It is more productive to make sure jurors know up front that some people are well suited to serve on one type of case and others are better suited to serve on a different type of case. Personal experiences and background are unique to each juror. If jurors understand the process this way, it will be less intimidating, and they will feel less threatened.

Once jurors are comfortable answering questions, lawyers must listen carefully to what is being expressed. They must ask follow-up questions. The issue isn't whether a juror has had experiences relevant to the case, but whether or how those experiences will impact the juror's ability to evaluate or weigh the evidence. Since fairness is the issue, follow-up is important.

Like all parts of trial, lawyers should do their best as effective communicators during jury selection. This is the only time in a trial when lawyers and jurors can engage in a two-way conversation. Lawyers should make eye contact with each juror. During questioning, it is important to include everyone. No one should feel left out.

The tone of the questioning should be respectful. If a juror has an unusual name or a name that is difficult to pronounce, a good lawyer will take a moment to learn it correctly. If a preliminary question calls for a show of hands, every juror with a hand up should be allowed to speak. It is alright for a lawyer to double check and make sure everyone got a chance to speak on the pending topic. It is human to lose your place or need to double-check. Jurors appreciate effort and sincerity.

The process of asking questions, listening to responses, and then asking follow-up questions is something which calls for skill and patience. The body language and facial expressions of jurors are also important. Before returning to counsel table, a lawyer should be satisfied that she has enough information about each juror to make intelligent use of challenges. There is never certainty. It is a process of intelligent "best guesses".

Observing other lawyers and sitting second chair is important, but practice is the only way to fully develop jury selection skills.

WHO ARE THESE PEOPLE (THE POTENTIAL JURORS)?

Coming into jury selection, most lawyers have limited information about the jurors. They also have limited time to review it and digest it. Standard jury questionnaires contain only the most basic biographical details. For example, a half-page form might have these details:

Name
Address
Name of spouse
Occupation
Prior jury service?

Friend or relative of law enforcement officer?

Prior litigant?

Witness or accused?

Special circumstances or hardship if asked to serve?

The questionnaire is just a starting point. Jury selection should be methodical and organized. One way of easing into the process is to flesh out more detail for the answers provided in the questionnaires. Most of these basic biographical details will not be embarrassing or controversial, so the jurors can begin in a comfort zone. It is also helpful to speak to each juror and learn something about them before moving on to case-specific subjects.

Answers on the questionnaires may be incomplete. If a juror lists his occupation as "retired", a logical follow-up would be,

"Mr. Gleason, I see that you are retired. What was your field before retiring?"

Lawyers should be polite and straightforward during jury selection. Jury selection is not a cocktail party or a lecture. Good lawyers avoid overly familiar or overly formal approaches.

"Ms. Robert, I see that you are a homemaker. Have you also worked outside the home?"

"Mr. Jones, what grade do you teach?"

"What subjects do you teach?"

"I see that your spouse is retired. What did your spouse do before retiring?"

"Ms. Nguyen, I see that you have served on a jury before. Was that here in Geeville?"

"Was that a civil case or a criminal case?"

"Were you the foreperson of the jury?"

Defense Counsel in a criminal case:

"Ms. Smith, I see that you checked the box about law enforcement. Do you have friends or family members in law enforcement?"
> (I have a neighbor)

"What agency is your neighbor with?"
> (She is with the city police)

"Do you sometimes talk with your neighbor about her job?"
> (Nothing specific)

"How often do the two of you visit?"
> (We go for walks on the weekends)

"Some of the witnesses in this trial will be from the Sherriff's Office. Do you know anyone who works in the Sherriff's Office?"
> (No)

"In your view, are law enforcement witnesses any different from other people who might testify?"
> (They probably come to court more often)

"Do you feel as if law enforcement witnesses would be more believable because of their career choice?"
> (No, I think it depends on the person)

After a discussion with one juror, other jurors may be interested in sharing their views on the same topic. For example:

"Let's go down the row so everyone can participate. Mr. Wolcott, do you think a law enforcement witness would automatically be more believable than a witness who had a different type of job?"
> (I think police officers are usually truthful, it's part of their job)

"Would you automatically give more weight to a police witness than a non-police witness?"

(I might give the police witness more weight)

"Would it be fair to say that the side without police witnesses might be starting out at a disadvantage?"
(I would try to be fair, but I think I would lean toward the police side of it)

"Ms. Blanding, how about you? Do you have views one way or the other?"

Plaintiff's counsel in a personal injury case:

"By a show of hands, how many of you have been in a traffic accident or had a family member involved in one?"
(several jurors raise hands)

"Let's start in the back row. Mr. Dean, how many accidents have you been involved in?"
(Just one)

"Was anyone hurt in the accident?"
(We were both injured, but it was his fault)

"Did either of you make a claim in the case?"
(My car was totaled, so we sued them)

"Did you settle the case, or did it go to court?"
(We settled)

"How did you feel about that experience?"
(I was satisfied)

"Is there anything about your experience with that traffic accident that would make it difficult for you to sit as a juror in this case?"
(No, I wouldn't have a problem with it)

"Mr. Keene, what are you studying at the University?"
(Engineering)

"What are your plans after you graduate?"
    (Not a clue)

"I see that you have been a witness in a case before. What type of case was it?"
    (Someone stole my boss's scooter and I had to give a deposition)

"What was that experience like?"
    (I just told the lawyers what I saw)

"Was that here in Tampa?"
    (No, it was in Jacksonville, about 3 years ago)

"Did the scooter case go to trial?
    (No, I think it settled out of court)

"Mr. Anderson, I see that you are a nurse. Can you tell us some more about your work?"
    (I work in the burn unit at University Hospital)

"How long have you worked in the burn unit?"
    (Two and a half years)

"Have you ever worked at North Hospital?"
    (No)

"Do you know any of the witnesses whose names were read in court this morning?"
    (No)

"Have you ever worked in the emergency room?"
    (Yes, during my training)

"Have you had patients with head trauma?
    (Yes)

As a nurse, have you ever had to testify in depositions or in trial?"
    (Not personally)

"Have some of your co-workers or friends had to testify?"
       (One of the nurses I work with had to give a deposition)

"Do you know what kind of case that was?"
       (I think it was a domestic battery)

"Ms. Blue, let me ask you the same question we asked down in the front row. How do you feel about giving a person money damages?"
       (I understand it. I think it's the only way to compensate a person)

"Mr. Hess, how about you? How do you feel about money damages?"

Defense counsel in a criminal trial:

"Ms. Hines, you mentioned earlier that you were a juror in a civil case. This case involves a criminal charge, with a higher burden of proof. Would that difference be important to you?"

"Would you be able to change gears from the greater weight standard to beyond a reasonable doubt?"

"In a criminal case, the state is the only party who has to present proof. Do you have feelings about that one way or the other?"

Lawyers must ask follow-up questions like those above, listen to the answers, and continue with more logical follow-up based on the facts and issues in the case. This is a way of getting to know and understand each juror to the extent possible in a courtroom setting. If a juror expresses views or relates experiences that suggest a bias in favor of the opposing party, it is also important to make a record.

Plaintiff's counsel in a medical malpractice trial:

"Before we move on, we would like to remind each of you that, if you need to tell us some things that are very personal, or we ask you a question that it is not comfortable to answer in front of a group, we will ask the Judge to allow a side bar. Can you work with us if we try to make everyone comfortable?"

"Ms. Ford, you mentioned that your husband had surgery three years ago. Are you comfortable telling us if it was elective surgery or otherwise?"

"So this was an emergency situation?"

"What hospital was your husband taken to?"

"How did the surgery go?"

"What are your feelings about the care and treatment your husband received?"

"Given that you feel your husband's doctor saved his life, would you have any difficulty serving as a juror in this type of case?"

"Do you view cosmetic surgery as different from other types of surgery?"

"Is it fair to say our client might have an uphill battle at the very outset?"

Defense counsel in a criminal trial:

"Because these are criminal charges, Mr. Smith is not required to present any evidence or call any witnesses. The constitution requires the state to prove criminal charges as opposed to requiring an accused person to prove innocence. Mr. Dorn, what do you think about that?"
> (I agree with it, I think the state should have the burden)

"Mr. Rice, how do you feel about it?"
> (I understand it's the law, but I assume he would want to testify on his own behalf)

"Is it fair to say you would prefer to hear his side of it?"
> (Yes, I think so)

"Would you feel a little cheated if he chose not to testify?"
> (I might, yes)

"If Mr. Smith doesn't present any evidence in the trial, is it fair to say that might influence your decision?"

    (I understand it's his right, but I think it would be a factor, yes)

"Alright. How about you, Ms. Fox? How do you feel about this issue?"

Defense counsel in a highly public, emotional case:

"Jury selection is not for lawyers on either side to make friends. We are here to find 12 jurors who can be fair. I am here to find 12 jurors who can be fair to my client."

    (going down the row) "Mr. Jones, is there anything about this case that causes you to feel like you could not be fair?"

"If you are called to serve in this case, the judge will instruct you that your verdict must be dispassionate—that you must set aside feelings of prejudice or sympathy toward either side. Ms. King, if you hear evidence in this case that causes you to feel anger or sympathy, will you be able to set those feelings aside?"

    (Yes, I can do that)

Listening is the key to understanding. As a skill, listening is often overlooked or taken for granted. Lawyers who develop this skill do better in jury selection for several reasons. They learn more about each juror. Because they learn more, they can follow up and develop the discussion topics in a richer way. Jurors appreciate lawyers who listen, so this skill is helpful when establishing trust. Trust leads to greater candor and willingness to share experiences and views. It also carries over as good will throughout the trial. Jurors reciprocate. They listen to the lawyer who listened to *them*.

IN JURY SELECTION, QUESTIONS SHOULD BE PHRASED IN A *NEUTRAL WAY.*

Jurors will volunteer information and opinions if (and only if) they feel comfortable. They will be candid about feelings or experiences close to the case when (and only when) they feel they are in a non-judgmental atmosphere. Jurors become silent and disengaged when they sense they may be subject to disdain or even ridicule. Questions should be phrased in a way that invites views from all sides. If jurors trust a lawyer to treat their individual experiences and views with respect, they are more likely to participate fully in the process.

Some lawyers approach jury selection with the goal of "educating" the jurors. Although this is a valid goal, it is secondary to the absolute need for lawyers to *become educated* about each potential juror on behalf of a client.

Here are some areas a lawyer might need to address with the secondary goal of educating or orienting the jurors to important concepts:

The burden of proof and who has it

The need to listen to the entire case before making decisions

The type of remedies or damages possible in the lawsuit

The fact that a key witness is a co-defendant or government informant

The fact that there will be very graphic or disturbing photos

The fact that there will be a mental health issue in the case

The fact that there will be a child witness in the case

These topics should be raised in the context of juror viewpoints: Are they familiar with the area or topic? Do they have a view on the topic? What is the view? Are they comfortable with the concept? Would it be difficult for some of the jurors to sit on a case or decide a case with this issue? Would a juror's personal experience or feeling on this issue make it difficult for him to follow the law, even with honest effort? Would a juror's profound personal experience cause her to favor one side over the other, even before hearing the case?

In any case, there will be jurors who will be unable or unwilling to decide the case based on the proof and the law. For these jurors, one party is at an automatic disadvantage. Lawyers must identify these jurors and ask that they be excused for cause. If the cause challenge is denied, a peremptory challenge must be used to protect the client's right to an impartial jury.

It is not proper for a party to seek a favorable commitment to a *verdict* during jury selection. It is proper and necessary to explore areas where potential jurors may be predisposed to the other side, or otherwise prevented from approaching the case with *fairness*. For example, a prosecutor needs to know if there are jurors who will *automatically* discount evidence from an informant. A defense attorney needs to know if there are jurors who will *automatically* give more weight to police witnesses than non-police witnesses. A plaintiff's lawyer needs to know whether potential jurors are philosophically opposed to the concept of pain and suffering awards.

Once the witnesses have been presented, jurors are free to weigh the evidence as they see fit. They can choose to believe or disbelieve any witness, and they can choose to accept or reject one side's proof or arguments in favor of another. At jury selection, the issue is whether one party is *starting* at a disadvantage. Jurors who will *automatically* favor one side over another before they have heard any evidence are subject to challenge for cause.

Lawyers should do the best possible job for their clients in jury selection. Once they are selected to serve, jurors are on the honor system. The verdict will be in their hands. The power is in their hands. Jurors deliberate and decide in the privacy of the jury room. They are shielded by law from compelled post-trial interviews. After trial, any discussion they have about their decisions must be voluntary.

The more attention given to the views and experiences of the jurors during jury selection, the better a lawyer's chance of establishing credibility for the duration of the trial. Some mistakes to avoid are:

Skipping over some jurors during the discussion
Being condescending
Being preachy
Asking questions in an adversarial way
Asking questions that have no value in the process (just being nosy)
Talking more than listening
Failing to listen to jurors when the other side is asking questions

There are also objectionable practices. These include:

Asking jurors to commit to a verdict
Asking jurors for a commitment to the client's side
Attempting to "pre-try" the case during jury selection
Bragging, discussing one's self or one's personal views
Attempts to curry favor, "chummy" talk, "speed dating"
Asking questions that suggest some of the laws in the case are bogus
Asking irrelevant or inflammatory questions
Exercising peremptory challenges solely on the basis of race or gender

Each case is different. There may be facts and issues that seem commonplace, but there will be others that are unique. The background of each juror is important in the context of the case. Who will the witnesses be? What issues will jurors have to address if chosen to decide the case?

Here are some topics that are important in various types of cases. How should a lawyer approach these topics in jury selection?

Firearms/ gun possession/gun rights/ self defense
Drug use/ illegal drugs/ addiction
Paid informants/ cooperating defendants
Alcohol use/ driving after drinking/ impairment
Domestic violence
The death penalty
Privacy
Mental illness/disability
Sexual abuse/child abuse
Money damages/ non-economic damages/pain and suffering award
Racial or ethnic prejudice
Sexual or gender orientation
Law and order/authority

To make people comfortable, it is helpful to introduce a topic by asking for a show of hands. For example:

"By a show of hands, how many of you drink alcoholic beverages?"

"How many of you serve alcohol in your home?"
     or

"Let's talk about traffic accidents. How many of you have been involved in an accident?"

"Okay, of those with their hands up, how many have been involved in an accident where someone got hurt?"

In some cases, there will be a need to address sensitive topics. Topics like intimate violence, racial discrimination, or child abuse often make jurors uncomfortable. Jurors are relative strangers brought together by summons to a very public setting. They may be reluctant to speak out about traumatic personal experiences or talk publicly about experiences of family members. They may be inhibited by court reporters and spectators. Lawyers must think of ways to allow jurors to express their views or relate experiences without embarrassment. These might include:

> Explaining that the process in not intended to embarrass anyone
> Asking the judge's permission to have the juror speak at sidebar
> Requesting individual (sequestered) voir dire on certain topics
> Submitting written questions in advance of court and then having individual
> follow-up

If stigma attaches to certain viewpoints, jurors will be less willing to speak candidly. If a lawyer signals that certain viewpoints are wrong or unacceptable, jurors will hold back. It is important to stress that unique personal experiences and feelings might make a juror less suited to hear a certain type of case (or better suited for a different case).

Lawyer to jurors early in the process:

> "There are no right or wrong answers during jury selection. We are not here to
> test you. We are not here to embarrass you. Jury selection is an important part
> of the trial for both sides, and we are here doing the best we can for our clients.
> We will be asking you questions, and we will listen to each of you with respect.
> Is that fair?"

Examples of possible questions in a racially charged case/case with concerns about prejudice:

> (This is a good time to request individual, sequestered voir dire)

> "Do you have friends or extended family members who are of a different race
> than you?"

> "Ms. Haines, what is the situation in your family?"

"How did you feel about your son marrying a person of a different race?"

"Mr. Joiner, in your workplace, are there people of different races or ethnic backgrounds?"

"Do you socialize with people who are a different race than you?"

"Do you belong to any organizations that advocate separation of people based on race or superiority of one race over another?"

"How do you feel about mixed race marriages?"

"Do you visit websites or participate in social media that endorses any sort of racial separation or ideas about racial superiority?"

"If any of the witnesses in this case are a different race than you, would you have difficulty weighing their credibility due to that difference?"

"Do you have any assumptions about a person's credibility based on race or ethnic background?"

"Our client is a different race than you. Do you think that difference, either consciously or unconsciously, would cause you to make any assumptions about whether she is guilty of a crime"?

"Do you have a feeling that people of a different race than you are more likely to commit crimes?"

"Would you hold someone of another race to a different standard of conduct?"

Straightforward questions are the best way of getting to the issues:

(Defense) "Ms. Green, would you be inclined to give more weight to a witness's testimony just because that witness was a police officer?"

(Defense) "This case involves the death of a child, so we want to give everyone a chance to answer this question. If you were to serve on the jury, would you feel under pressure to convict? Mr. King, do you think you would feel pressure because of that?"

(Prosecutor) "Two of the witnesses we will call in this trial have plea agreements. Without hearing anything else, is there anyone who feels they would automatically reject what these witness say?"

HOW SHOULD CAUSE AND PEREMPTORY CHALLENGES BE EXERCISED?
CAUSE CHALLENGES.

Cause challenges protect the constitutional underpinning of the trial. A litigant should not have to overcome bias or partiality before the evidence is even presented. Pre-disposed jurors threaten the right to a fair trial. Doubts about the ability of a juror to be impartial should be resolved in favor of the party disadvantaged by the juror's predisposition.

To successfully challenge a juror for cause, a lawyer must establish bias *on the record*. Reasonable doubts about the ability of a juror to be impartial usually appear with follow-up questions. For example, Mr. Rice in the earlier example would be challenged by defense counsel because his answers indicate he would not be able to honor the burden of proof.

For this reason, it is important to create an atmosphere of trust during jury selection. Jurors need to understand it's okay to be open about bias. Jurors are more willing to speak with candor when it is apparent they are in a judgment-free zone. It is up to lawyers to create that zone, where relative strangers feel comfortable discussing their experiences, attitudes, and beliefs.

All challenges should be made at sidebar or in chambers, beyond the hearing of jurors.

Cause challenges are based on the right to a fair trial, so an arbitrary limit on their number would be improper. If a cause challenge is unsuccessful, the issue should be preserved for appeal by using a peremptory challenge to remove the juror, exhausting any remaining peremptory challenges, and asking the judge for additional peremptory challenges. The panel should be accepted subject to objection based on the denied cause challenge and additional efforts to seat acceptable jurors.

Among the remaining jurors, who will be most receptive to the client's case? Are there jurors on the panel who are more likely to identify with or relate to the other side? Are there worrisome jurors who were either challenged unsuccessfully for cause, or just give reason for concern based on their answers? Are there jurors who gave acceptable answers, but demonstrated through tone or body language that they are not happy with the lawyer or the client?

Unlike cause challenges, peremptory challenges may be exercised for any reason, and lawyers are not required to state a reason on the record. An exception exists where one side objects to the exercise of a peremptory challenge by the other side under *Batson v. Kentucky*[3] and its progeny. The Supreme Court has held that preemptory challenges may not be used to exclude citizens from jury service based solely on race or gender.

Peremptory challenges are limited in number by statute or rule, so they should be exercised thoughtfully. The best use of peremptory challenges is educated guess-work. For obvious reasons, peremptory challenges should first be used to remove jurors who were unsuccessfully challenged for cause. Once all challenges have been exhausted, a lawyer may need to ask the judge for additional peremptory challenges to preserve the record for appeal.

Lawyers should be permitted to consider the jury as a unit rather than piecemeal, so strikes should be permitted up to the time the jury is sworn to hear the case.

ALTERNATE JURORS.

Jurisdictions have various procedures for selecting and, if needed, seating alternate jurors. Sometimes alternates are optional. Broadly, the party with the burden is better off with fewer jurors if given a choice, and the party with no burden is better off with a larger number (more potential for a hold-out).

---

3   476 U.S. 79 (1986).

    Outline for jury selection (topics and phrasing)

    Questionnaires (obtain them as soon as they are available)

    Specific follow-up based on questionnaires (make notes as soon as possible)

    Case law relating to jury selection

Lawyers who put thought and energy into jury selection get better results than those who pull a script out of a notebook the night before. At this stage of the case, there is nothing in between the lawyers and the jurors. The evidence isn't in the room yet. The witnesses are not there either.

If a lawyer is arrogant, boring, or perfunctory, it sets a negative tone for the entire trial. If a lawyer is engaged, straightforward, and mindful, jurors are more likely to start off in the same mode.

Tell the story.

Use the words and language of the story.

Use the natural themes in the story.

Adopt or neutralize the other side's facts where possible.

Be a narrator (not a preacher, a professor, or a law clerk).

Do not be tentative, vague, or evasive.

Let the jurors know what they will be asked to decide.

If *both* sides have done a good job in jury selection, jurors come into the courtroom on the day of opening statements in a receptive mood. Even if they come in with an idea about who should win, their positions may shift dramatically as they listen to opening statements. Many lawyers view opening statement as the place where cases are won or lost. Although each part of a trial has an important purpose, a strong, fact-rich opening statement may give one side enough momentum to carry the case all the way to a favorable verdict.

OPEN THE CASE WITH THE CLIENT'S STORY.

Tell the jurors what happened. Jurors want to know the story before they hear the witnesses. They want to know what to anticipate. Good lawyers tell the story of the case from the perspective of their clients. They don't help the opponent by dwelling on the opponent's facts. They don't apologize for bad facts. They don't waste the time and attention span of jurors with long-winded introductions or sermons about the trial process. They don't present the case as complicated or difficult.

It is a lawyer's job to make the case understandable. If anything needs to be "translated" from an obscure form to an easy form, the lawyer must accept responsibility for getting that done. What happened? How do we know it happened? Why does it matter? What will the jurors need to do with the case after they have heard all the evidence?

Good lawyers capture the key pro-client events in the opening. They present them in a way that is interesting and appealing. The people in the case become real. The client's story becomes important. The issues become clear. When the opening is over, the jurors are ready to see and hear that same story in the evidence. They want to decide the case in a way that validates the compelling opening story. Jurors will measure the case against the openings of both sides as the trial progresses.

Lawyers should have something of value to tell jurors in opening statement. This is true whether the client has a burden of proof or not. For example, a criminal defense attorney may tell a shadow story as opposed to the prime story of the prosecution. The defense attorney may narrate the underside of the case, exposing weaknesses in the evidence and credibility problems of prosecution witnesses, like a good *film noir.* There may be a story *within* a story. In a reasonable doubt case, the defense opening has very little to do with the client, but it is still the client's story in the context of the case.

In opening, lawyers should be permitted to include any information they have a good faith intention of offering into evidence. They can also refer to information they anticipate the opponent will offer, with the exception that prosecutors should only discuss prosecution evidence during opening. This is because the defendant has no burden of proof in a criminal trial. The defendant is not required to commit in advance to presenting *anything*, so it is not proper for the prosecution to address defense evidence in opening. In unusual cases where the defendant has an affirmative defense *requiring* some evidence (insanity), the lawyers may want to address the scope of opening with the judge.

Prosecution in criminal trial:

Members of the Jury, appearances can deceive. Sometimes things are not what they seem.

It's 2017. Three days after Christmas, on Walnut Street, a college student is out on the sidewalk stretching and warming up, getting ready for an early morning run. The student is staying at the home of his roommate's parents. He will soon be on his way back to school after the winter break. At the house across the street, a man and a woman are packing a car. The man comes out of the garage and puts a green plastic trash bag in the trunk of a grey car. The student notices the man has a bandage around the palm of his right hand, and it is partly red. He describes it as the color of blood. The woman comes out the front door of the house and puts some clothes in the front seat. The woman goes back into the house and comes out with a paper bag and puts it into a garbage can at the curb. The man and the woman go back into the house for a moment, and then the woman comes back outside. As the student begins his run, he notices the woman takes the paper bag back out of the garbage can and walks toward the car. When the student comes back from his run about twenty minutes later, the garage door is closed, and the car is gone.

Fast forward to January 9th. The police are on Walnut Street. A woman has reported that her co-worker hasn't shown up at work for several days and won't answer her phone or come to her door. The police enter the house and find Barbara Reese. She appears to have been struck with a heavy object. She has been dead for several days. Barbara's co-worker tells police that Barbara's husband, who is out of the country on business, has been trying unsuccessfully to reach Barbara. He has called, texted, and e-mailed.

The husband returns to Walnut Street and makes a statement to reporters at WGJG. The statement is televised. The husband is tearful and appears distraught over the violent death of his wife. He states over and over that his wife had no enemies.

Back to the student, who is now at school. His roommate tells him about the news from Walnut Street. The student goes on the internet. The student sees an image of Barbara Reese's husband. The student immediately recognizes the husband as the man who was packing the grey car on Walnut Street three days after Christmas. The husband was the man who had the bandage

around the palm of his right hand. The student contacts the police department. Soon afterward, the student identifies the woman he saw on Walnut
Street as Barbara Reese's co-worker.

All the calls and texts to Barbara's cell phone from her husband's cell
phone after December 28th come from out of state except one. One of the calls
pinged off a cell tower near the co-worker's house. That house is three miles
away from the Reese's home.

The husband's blood is on the closet doorknob in the room where Barbara
was found. It is also on the edge of a table near the garage door. It is also
on the inside edge of the trunk lid of a grey Toyota sedan rented by the co-
worker two days after Christmas.

The husband is Gerald Reese, the defendant, seated at counsel table, here.

The co-worker is Gretchen Forsythe. Ms. Forsythe has entered into a plea
agreement in this case. She will testify in this trial. The defendant and Ms.
Forsythe were having an affair. It started in late 2016. Ms. Forsythe helped the
defendant kill his wife on December 27th, at the Reese home. You will see the
hammer that was used to kill Barbara Reese. Barbara's blood was found on
the hammer.

We will prove beyond a reasonable doubt that Barbara Reese's death was
pre-meditated, and that Gerald Reese is the person who carried it out.

At the end of this trial, we will ask you to find the defendant guilty of first
degree murder.

Appearances can deceive.

Plaintiff's lawyer in wrongful termination trial:

Two years ago, Shelli Green was fired by her employer, the defendant, Craft
Zone. We are here to show you why she was fired and why her firing was
unlawful.

Ms. Green was fired four months after she became pregnant. She was in
a brief relationship with her supervisor's brother-in-law, and the relationship
resulted in a pregnancy. During the trial, several witnesses will help you
understand what Ms. Green's supervisor knew and when she knew it.

You will see a series of e-mails between Mary Havers, the supervisor, and
John Rentz, the personnel manager. Mr. Rentz will explain parts of the e-mails
that are not already clear.

Sydney Merrill, Ms. Green's co-worker, was present during two conversations Mary Havers had about Shelli Green. These conversations took place on March 3rd and March 31st. On March 3rd, Ms. Merrill witnessed a loud argument between Mary Havers and her brother-in-law, Dan Mayo. The argument took place in the employee parking lot at Craft Zone. The argument was about Ms. Green. Ms. Havers expressed anger at her brother-in-law for having an affair with Ms. Green. She said, "You are going to pay for it for the next eighteen years." On March 31st, Mary Havers told John Rentz that she was in a hurry to fire Ms. Green. Her exact words were, "I've got to fire her before she starts to show."

Ms. Green tried to keep her pregnancy a secret. She will tell you that. She even told John Rentz she was not pregnant. She acted offended when he asked her about it. She was hopeful that she could obtain a transfer to a Craft Zone store in a nearby city where she had more family support. She did not want to be the subject of gossip.

Everyone agrees Shelli Green was fired on April 3rd. Everyone agrees she was pregnant at the time she was fired. The defendant will present a different set of reasons for Shelli Green's firing. We expect Mary Havers to say that Shelli Green was fired for poor work performance. Witnesses from the defendant's own personnel department will tell you that Shelli Green was an excellent employee. Co-workers will tell you she was an excellent employee.

You will hear the all the evidence, and you will decide why Shelli Green was fired. We will prove to you she was fired because she was pregnant.

That is against the law, and that is why we are here today.

When the defendants fired Shelli Green, they broke the law.

Plaintiff opening on damages:

Gus Stanford had to have four surgeries. He now visits the pain management clinic every week. He can no longer play golf, something he has done since he was a little boy. He can no longer take Belle, his wife of 43 years, dancing. He can no longer go on hikes with his son, who lives in the mountains. He has lost all of this. He is a different person because of this crash. We will try to give you a picture of what Gus was like before this happened.

Defense in criminal trial:

This is not a "whodunit". This is a "why". This is Austin Goodrich (lawyer standing by client). Austin is 36 years old. He suffers from severe post-traumatic stress disorder, also called PTSD. As a marine, Austin served two tours of duty in the Middle East. He was diagnosed with PTSD in 2008 after being badly injured in combat.

Austin was defending himself against Lawrence Jones and two of Lawrence's friends when this happened.

Austin was at home when this happened.

Lawrence Jones is on probation. Buck Anderson, another state witness you heard about a few moments ago, has a pending case in the prosecutor's office. Lawrence and Buck have reasons to slant things a certain way. You will hear the reasons during their testimony, and you will be permitted to consider all of them when you are developing a picture of what happened.

On September 7th of last year, around supper time, Austin was sitting in his living room replacing the batteries in a wall clock. As Austin worked on the clock, Lawrence Jones and two of his friends started setting off fireworks in a field between Austin's house and the highway. Austin's Nephew, Jamie Goodrich, was out in the back yard when the fireworks began. Jamie went immediately into the house to check on his Uncle. Jamie found Austin curled up in a fetal position under the covers of his bed.

The fireworks continued. Jamie got the dogs inside the house and closed the windows.

Austin Goodrich and Lawrence Jones do not get along. Lawrence has threatened Austin in front of other people on two separate occasions. Lawrence has also threatened to harm Austin's nephew and his dogs.

The fireworks got closer and closer to Austin's house that evening. At one point, Lawrence Jones was up at Austin's window, taunting him. Austin and Jamie heard Lawrence's friend, Buck Anderson, yell, "spray him!" Jamie was about to call the police when Austin came out of the bedroom and ran out the back door with a shotgun. He fired it in the direction of Lawrence Jones's SUV. One of the bullets struck a wheel rim and then hit Lawrence in the shin. Jamie heard Lawrence yell, and he immediately called 911. Jamie was able to talk his Uncle back into the house and into the kitchen, where they waited for the ambulance. Lawrence's injury was not life-threatening.

When Officer Forsyth arrived, Austin was on the floor in the bedroom. Austin was shaking so badly that three officers had to pick him up off the floor.

Sydney Morris is a doctor who specializes in the diagnosis and treatment of post- traumatic stress disorder. Dr. Morris will explain what PTSD is, and help you understand the ways it affects people who suffer from it. This will be helpful when you are considering the behavior of Lawrence and his friends, the way Austin perceived it, and the way he reacted.

Austin Goodrich was defending his nephew, his home, his dogs, and his life that night.

At the end of this trial, we will ask you to find him not guilty.

Defense in personal injury trial:

Henry Bach stayed in his lane. He was on the way to pick up his daughters from swim practice. He was early. He stayed inside the speed limit.

Henry drops the girls off and picks them up at the same times twice a week.

We don't know why the plaintiff's car veered into Henry's lane. Henry was about midway between mile marker 259 and mile marker 260 when the plaintiff's car crossed into the center lane from the right. There was heavy traffic in all three lanes that afternoon.

Pat Weaver was in the car behind Henry's van. Pat will tell you that the van did not move outside the lane. There were several cars, at least three, on the entrance ramp, merging from the far right, when this happened.

Freda Reynolds was a passenger in Pat's car. Freda lives in Scotland now, so you will see and hear her recorded testimony. Freda saw the first car in what she calls "the pipe line" cut the plaintiff car off on the curve at mile marker 259.

This is a sad case, because the plaintiff was badly injured. As we discussed in jury selection, it is natural to have sympathy when someone gets hurt. People don't lose their ability to feel sympathy when they get selected for jury service, but they promise, as you have, to set those feelings aside so they can address the issues in the trial.

The issue you are here to decide is fault. The plaintiffs cannot prevail unless they can meet their burden of proving Henry Bach did something wrong.

Henry stayed inside his lane, and he stayed inside the speed limit. At the end of this trial, we will ask you to find in his favor, not liable.

Prosecution in criminal trial:

Members of the jury, on June 3rd, between 10:40pm and 11:23pm, the defendant, Ellen Grady, sent eleven text messages to her husband. The first text message said, "I am going to kill myself". The last text message, sent at 11:23pm, said, "Free at last". Moments after that message, the defendant put her foot all the way down on the gas pedal of her Ford Explorer and crashed into the Honda Civic in front of her.

The defendant was on the North Bridge when this happened. The force of the crash lifted the back of the Honda Civic and caused it to flip sideways. The Honda went through the rails. The Honda was pulled from the water by a crane 2 hours later. The driver, a 32-year old man named Jessie Kramer, was dead. Mr. Kramer was unable to get out of his car. He drowned.

The defendant was taken by ambulance to Memorial Hospital. She survived her injuries. Life is full of irony. The defendant was not successful in killing herself, but she did kill someone else. Life is stranger than fiction.

Eleven text messages. "You are going to be sorry." "Finished." "Get what you deserve." At 11:07pm, "you ruined everything." At 11:23pm, "Free at last." You will see all the messages during this trial.

Ezra Liddell is an investigator with the State Highway Patrol. He has 23 years of experience investigating traffic crashes. He got to the crash shortly after the defendant was taken to the hospital. He will tell you what he did in this case and what his conclusions were. He will explain how he works. Investigator Liddell concluded the Honda Civic was going about 30 miles an hour when it was struck from the rear by the defendant's Explorer. He will also explain how fast the Explorer was going at the time of impact.

We are here today because an innocent life was taken by this defendant. She took someone else's life. We will prove to you beyond a reasonable doubt that the defendant is guilty of 2d degree murder.

Defense in same trial:

Ellen Grady was not trying to commit suicide. She was leaving her husband, as she had several times over a rocky 17-year marriage. Ellen and her husband,

Ian, dealt with their problems in a very public way. Over the years, friends and co-workers watched as the couple argued, split up, and reunited.

On June 3rd, Ellen was on her way to her sister's house in Jackson. She drove onto the North Bridge around 11:30pm. The bridge is almost a mile long. As she crossed the bridge, Ellen came upon a car stopped in the road. This will be an issue in the trial-- whether the Honda was moving or completely stopped at the time Ellen's car hit the back of it. The force of the impact caused Ellen's gas pedal to jam.

A 911 call was placed by another driver at 11: 35. Paramedics arrived at 11:48.

Ellen was wearing her seatbelt. She was still belted in, unconscious, when the paramedics got to the car. There was a package of dog treats in the car. Ellen often brought dog treats to her sister's house for her sister's terrier.

As we discussed during jury selection, this is not a civil case. The prosecution has a burden on each element of the charge beyond and to the exclusion of every reasonable doubt.

June 3rd was a very, very sad day in the lives of two families. The trial will not be about whether there was a tragedy. The trial will be about whether there is proof, a special kind of proof—proof beyond a reasonable doubt, that a crime occurred.

In this trial, we will see what we already know, that tragedy happens without crime.

Lawyers who migrate from the story narrative into argument may draw an objection. The jurors have not yet heard the evidence, so argument about the relative merit of each side's case is premature. The judge decides whether a lawyer is overly argumentative in opening. Judges have a broad range of discretion in this area, so practice varies. If an "argumentative" objection is sustained, a lawyer can recover from the objection by moving back to the *facts* underlying the argument.

For example:

"Members of the jury, you can't trust what John Phillips tells you, because his self-serving audit was compromised before Mr. Stephens ever saw it"-

"Objection, argumentative."

"Sustained."

"John Phillips will admit that he went over the quarterly audit with his girlfriend's father. His girlfriend's father also works for the company. The couple are engaged. Phillips and his future father-in-law made three changes in the auditor's report two days before it was submitted to Del Stephens."

How does a good opening sound? It sounds as if the lawyer knows what happened. How does a good opening look? It looks interesting.

USE THE WORDS AND LANGUAGE OF THE CASE.

Jurors revisit opening statements as they listen to witnesses and study evidence. They test what the lawyers have told them against the proof. Highly credible opening statements survive this scrutiny. Lawyers who stay true to the evidence in opening statements build trust and credibility with jurors as the trial continues. Direct quotes from key players in the case are powerful openers for this reason. Themes which echo as the testimony comes in are powerful.

(Prosecutor) "I think I hit a deer". That's what the defendant said to his landlord when he got home from Somerset at 2am on April 4th. "I think I hit a deer."

(Defense lawyer) "This case is about payback."

(Plaintiff's lawyer) "This case is about calculated risk. The risk is what might happen without a guard on this cutting blade (showing picture). This case is about the cost per unit versus the small number of anticipated accidents. Members of the jury, the defendants took that risk, and they lost."

(Medical malpractice defense lawyer) "People lose their battle with heart disease every day. In this case the plaintiff, a beloved husband and father, lost his battle after a brave fight and several weeks in the hospital. Dr. Casey did everything he could to help this terrific man, who was his patient."

Bad facts should be handled gracefully during openings. If they *must* be acknowledged for the sake of credibility, they should be mentioned without apology. Jurors can sense fear. If a lawyer is afraid of the other side's facts, the client's position is weakened.

> "Mr. Barnes is not proud of the way he acted that night. He did not handle his anger well. He will explain what he did and why he did it."

> "We agree that the breathing tube became dislodged, and this was not noticed until Medics Johnson and Grey got Mr. Lane out of the ambulance. The issue here that is *why* Mr. Lane died. It was the overdose-- 80 milligrams of oxycodone, that killed Mr. Lane."

USE THE THEMES IN THE CASE.

If there is a favorable theme running through the case, jurors should hear it in the opening. A strong theme can rally the jurors and help them develop an attachment to the client's side of the case. Sometimes themes can be found in the words of key players. Direct quotes are powerful. Sometimes themes are best expressed in a single word. Themes can be explicit or implicit. The case dictates the theme and the best way to express it.

EXAMPLES OF THEMES.

Prosecutor in a bribery/official misconduct trial:

> *No one* is above the law.

Defense in a civil trial:

> The Plaintiff is an angry man. He's angry, and he's blaming someone else for what *he* caused.

Defense in a homicide trial:

> This case is about mental illness. It's a tragic case. It's a tragic story. To understand what happened on December 3rd of last year, we must understand Julian

Smith's world. From the time he was a teenager, Julian has lived in a strange and frightening world.

Prosecutor in a homicide trial:

This case is about love, money, and murder.

Plaintiff in a civil rights trial:

This case is about police, power, and prejudice.

Defense in a drug trafficking trial:

Fact, or fiction? Members of the jury, in this trial, *you* will decide. You will hear, see, and decide: fact, or fiction?

Plaintiff in an action against city officials:

What did they know, and when did they know it?

Plaintiff in a personal injury trial:

The Defendant took a chance. She gambled. She misjudged. She lost. Mr. Jones's children are now paying for that loss.

More themes and subthemes:

Abuse of power
What you see is what you get. If it walks like a duck and quacks like a duck...
Blood is thicker than water
Revenge
Jealousy
Instinct
Self-preservation
Wanting something that does not belong to you
Envy
Courage and bravery

Selling out

Selling your soul to the devil

Addiction

Powerlessness

Helplessness

Getting what you paid for

Willful blindness

Appearances can deceive

Nobody's perfect

No good deed goes unpunished

Loyalty

Devotion

Blind devotion

Fool me once, shame on you. Fool me twice.....

Skeletons in the closet

Family secrets

Sugar-coating

Lies in disguise

If the shoe fits, wear it

Look behind the façade

BE A NARRATOR.

People love good stories. They love exciting stories. They anticipate the ending—what will happen? Jurors bring anticipation into the courtroom. They don't want to be preached at. They don't want to be tested. They don't want to work too hard to understand what is being said or why it is important.

A good lawyer *narrates* the case for the jurors. Narrators have a kind of credibility that transcends other public speaking. Think of a Greek Chorus. Think of classic children's stories like *A Christmas Carol*[4] or *The Wizard of Oz*[5]. Narrators have cultural authority.

In opening statements, jurors gravitate toward the side with the best narrator. They appreciate the side with a genuine and compelling human story to tell.

---

4   Charles Dickens, 1843.

5   L. Frank Baum, 1900.

They pull away from the side that makes them feel as if they are getting a fast sell or a scratch-and-dent bargain.

A good story is easy to follow. It is not bloated with incidental information. At opening, jurors don't yet know what will be important in the case, so they try to absorb everything they hear. Good openers give the key facts and important details. They avoid areas of uncertainty. They avoid over-explaining. To the extent possible, they let the facts speak for themselves.

If permitted, lawyers should consider using exhibits during opening. Most judges permit lawyers to use exhibits in opening if the foundation or admissibility is not in controversy. However, an exhibit should not be used as a crutch. The story should stand on its own.

Examples:

> (Holding an endotracheal tube) "Members of the Jury, this is a breathing tube. When someone needs help to breathe, this simple tube is inserted through the mouth, the back of the throat, the vocal chords, and down the windpipe. Oxygen is then provided through the tube. This tube saves lives".

> (Picture of wrecked car on screen) "This is Mr. Duffy's car."

> (Image of a human spine) Ladies and Gentlemen, this is a human spine. This area here, between the 6th and 7th vertebrae, is where your attention will be focused during the trial."

Good narrators do not preach at their audience. In the courtroom, the audience is the jury. The dynamic between a lawyer and the jury is special. Jurors should feel empowered as opposed to pressured. Jurors want to be captivated, or at least *interested*, and not lectured. They don't want to hear a lot of legal terminology. They don't want to miss important facts while they are hung up on a confusing opening. It is the lawyers' job to make the case understandable and the issues clear.

EVERYTHING THE JURORS HEAR IN OPENING SHOULD BE
STATED WITH CONFIDENCE AND CLARITY. NOTHING SHOULD
BE TENTATIVE, VAGUE, OR EVASIVE.

It is not necessary to include every possible bit of admissible information in an opening statement. Lawyers sometimes give the opponent a new advantage by including too much information in the front end of the trial. Opponents can adjust, amend, and plan to counter based on overly informative openings. This risk can be minimized by doing a complete but thoughtfully simple opening. Rich detail, limited by importance, is another way to think of opening.

It is damaging to present the client's story in a tentative or evasive manner. Jurors notice evasive maneuvers. The best practice is to choose safe, clear, positive story facts and lay them out with simple grace.

LET THE JURORS KNOW WHAT THEY WILL HAVE TO DECIDE.

Is the case about what happened, or why it happened? Is it about both? Will the jurors need to decide more than one thing? What will their role be? Before they begin hearing evidence, the jurors should know what is required at the end. Some cases call for multiple decisions. Some only call for one.

No matter how well lawyers organize witnesses and evidence, the story comes to jurors in fragments. Jurors can fit the bits and pieces of the story together better and follow all the "threads" if they understand what they have to do with the case at the end. It is not important to be clever in the opening. It is important to make the issues clear and understandable.

This should be done without abandoning the story in favor of the law. It should be kept simple.

Some cases are like mystery novels. They are "whodunits". In other cases, the issue is what happened as opposed to who was involved. Some cases are all about the "why" (causation).

Direct Examination: The Client's Story

Tell the client's story through direct examination.

Allow jurors to use visual sense during direct examination.

Empower the witnesses who know the story.

In trial, direct examination is where the proof lives. Witnesses supply all the bits and pieces of the story that was promised during opening statement. The direct examiner should use "prompts" or simple, open-ended questions that are easy for the witness and the jurors to understand.

Good direct examinations look deceptively easy. The direct examiner is saying very little. Instead, he is helping the witnesses in his client's case-in-chief by conducting a special type of *interview* with each one.

Listening is an essential component of direct examination. The content and phrasing of each question should flow from the witness's last answer, in a logical sequence. A good direct examiner listens to each answer as if she doesn't know how the story ends. As the interview progresses, the jurors should learn more and more, as if the witness is filling in a canvas or completing a short story.

If the direct examination is poorly organized or full of unfamiliar words, the jurors have a harder time following the story. If important parts of the story are glossed over or too much time is spent on unimportant details, jurors may become frustrated. If the questions and answers do not seem to "match up", jurors may become disengaged. They may lose interest.

A good direct examiner *enables* her witnesses. With a series of simple, well-organized questions, most witnesses can provide the facts needed to prove the client's case. Some witnesses need more encouragement than others. Some witnesses are easier to understand than others. Good direct examiners are flexible enough to adapt the interview based on the witness and make the best possible presentation with each individual.

It is not interesting or effective to watch a lawyer move mechanically down a prepared list of questions. Instead, the lawyer should know the case well enough to do a "live interview" with the witness. If an outline is necessary, it should be used as a checklist and not as a script. The story of the case should flow clearly and logically from the witness.

Lawyers face challenges in direct examinations.

Witnesses are sometimes overly anxious. Some are very nervous. Most people have little or no practice as a witness. Few people find themselves in a courtroom, under oath, answering questions about a traumatic event. Most people go for a lifetime without ever appearing in a courtroom. Those who do may be unhappy about being a witness. They may be difficult or uncooperative. Witnesses are sometimes distracted. They sometimes feel guilty or embarrassed. Other witnesses are too willing to testify. They may blurt out harmful or irrelevant information. They may irritate or alienate the jurors. They may have their own agenda.

People relate information a little differently each time they tell about something they know. Sometimes the answers do not "line up" with the precise question asked. Witnesses sometimes unknowingly open the door to harmful information by straying too far from a proper question. Lawyers should go over direct examination questions with their witnesses before trial. The witnesses should be familiar with the subjects that will be covered.

During testimony, the direct examiner should avoid interrupting the witness unless it is necessary. Interruptions are frustrating for witnesses and jurors. Unlike the lawyers, the jurors are hearing the witnesses for the first time. Jurors want to feel as if they are getting the whole picture. Interruptions are distracting. Interruptions may also cause witnesses to lose a train of thought and forget important details.

In limited circumstances, it *is* necessary for a lawyer to interrupt his own witness. If the witness is heading into a mistrial, an interruption is preferable. If the witness is about to open the door to otherwise inadmissible material, an interruption is preferable.

Some witnesses have a habit of running on or drifting away from the questions. These witnesses should be instructed before trial on the need to answer specific questions and keep the answers focused. There are risks associated with volunteering information, and most cooperative witnesses will refrain from volunteering information if they understand it will hurt the case. When specific evidence has been excluded by pretrial rulings, lawyers should make sure their witnesses understand not to say things which may result in a mistrial or reversal.

EXAMPLES OF DIRECT EXAMINATION.

Good Morning. Please tell us your name.

Ms. Spencer, do you live in Geeville?

How long have you lived here?

Did you attend school here?

Where did you go to school?

After you graduated from Geeville High School, what did you do?

Are you working now?

Do you have children?

How old is your son?

Where does your son go to school?

Is Geeville Academy in Acme County, Florida?

Was your son attending Geeville Academy in February, 2017?

How did your son get to the Academy each morning?

Did you drive your son to the Academy on February 7, 2017?

I would like to talk about that morning, February 7[th.]

What time did you arrive at the Academy?

How is it that you know the time?

What radio program are you referring to?

What time did the program come on?

Where did you drop your son off once you arrived?

Once your son got out of the car, where did he go?

What did you do after your son walked into the building?

Please tell us what you saw as you pulled out of the circular drive.

Where was the red car when you saw it hit the child?

How far was your car from the red car?

What was the next thing that happened after the car hit the child?

What did you do after you ran over to the child?

Did the child move?

Did the child say anything while you were waiting?

How long was it before emergency medical services arrived?

During those 8 or 9 minutes, did anyone else come over to where you were waiting with the child?

What happened when the medics arrived?

Ms. Spencer, I want to ask you more about the red car now.

Could you see how many people were in the red car?

How many people were in the car?

Were you able to see the driver of the car as you came out of the circular drive?

How far were you from the driver's side of the red car at that moment?

Do you know the person who was driving the red car on February 7?

Who was driving?

Please look around the courtroom. Do you see the person who was driving the red car at Geeville Academy on February 7th?

Please point to the person and describe the clothing the person is wearing.

Is the person you have identified also the person you know as John Blue?
 (witness is tendered for cross examination)

Another example of direct examination:

Please tell us your name.

How old are you, Jason?

Where do you go to school?

What grade are you in?

Do you know a person named Charles Cooper?

How do you know Charles?

Is there another name you know Charles by?

Is that the name you use?

Do you know what grade Charlie is in?

How well do you know Charlie?

How long have you been good friends?

When you say you met in middle school, what school was that?

So how many years have you and Charlie been friends?

Jason, let's turn our attention to October 6th of last year. Do you recall that date?

Where were you on the morning of October 6th?

Is that the same high school that Charlie attends?

Did you see Charlie that morning?

When did you first see him that morning?

What time did study hall begin?

Where were you sitting in relation to Charlie?

Was there anyone between you and Charlie at the table?

What was Charlie wearing during study hall?

Did Charlie have any sort of coat or jacket on?

Did you see any sort of coat or jacket around Charlie in the study hall?

What was Charlie doing during study hall?

As he was seated at the table, did Charlie have anything in his hands?

How long was the study hall that morning?

At any point during that hour, did Charlie ever leave the table?

Jason, did you see a gun at the table where you and Charlie were sitting on the morning of October 6th?

Did you see any sort of weapon at the table that morning?

Did you see Charlie holding or touching anything at the table other than the laptop?

When study hall was over, where did you go?

Did you see where Charlie went?

Jason, did you see Charlie Cooper at any point on the morning of October 6th with a gun?
　　　　　(witness is tendered for cross examination)

A segment of fast-action direct:

Mr. Churchill, let's go moment by moment at this point.

You are on the lake. What kind of boat is it?

How many people are on board?

Who is driving?

Who is skiing?

When do you see the 2d boat?

Where is it coming from?

How fast is the 2d boat going?

How fast is your boat going?

What happens at the first marker?

Where does your boat end up?

Another example of direct examination:

Mr. Paul, please introduce yourself.

Where do you work?

How long have you worked at the Mill?

What are your duties there?

Who is your supervisor?

Was Sam Jepson your supervisor on April 7, 2017?

Mr. Paul, is there a retention pond at the mill?

Where is the retention pond?

Is there anything surrounding the retention pond?

Let the record reflect I am showing defense counsel plaintiff's exhibit B.

May I approach the witness, Your Honor?
          (showing exhibit)

Mr. Paul, I am showing you plaintiff's exhibit B for identification purposes. Do you recognize exhibit B?

How do recognize it?

What is it?

Is exhibit B a fair picture of the way the retention pond looked on April 7th, 2017?

We offer exhibit B into evidence as plaintiff's exhibit 2.
          (exhibit admitted without objection)

May we publish exhibit 2 by using a digital version?
          (exhibit published on large screen)

Mr. Paul, what is this bar-type object on the right side of exhibit 2?

Is the gate opened or closed in this picture?

How does this gate open and close?

Who has the access code for this gate?

Is there also a manual way to open the gate?

Are there any other gates or openings in this fence?

What would you have to do to access the pond from the south side?

Are there rules about the gate?

What are the rules?

How did you learn these rules?

Where are the rules posted?

Let's turn our attention to April 7th, 2017:

What time did you get to work on April 7th?

How do you know the time you arrived?

When you got there, did you notice anything about the gate at the retention pond?

How did you notice?

What did you do when you noticed the gate open?

Were you able to get the gate closed that morning?

Mr. Paul, did you tell anyone about the problem with the gate?

Who did you tell?

Where was Mr. Jepson when you told him about the gate?

Was anyone else there when you told Mr. Jepson?

What did you do after this conversation?

Were you ever asked to do anything else about the gate?
           (witness tendered for cross examination)

DIRECT EXAMINATION QUESTIONS SHOULD BE OPEN-ENDED.

Effective direct examination questions are drafted with these words:

Who
What
Where
When
Why
How

Describe

Tell us

These words are simple prompts. They *enable* a witness to give key story facts and details. In a transcript of a good direct examination, the questions are simple. Most of the client's story is in the answers. The story facts and details come from the witness (not the lawyer).

Direct exam questions should usually call for *factual* responses and, when helpful, descriptive details. *Feelings* are only relevant in specific circumstances. In some cases, it will be relevant that a victim or defendant felt fear. Feelings are relevant to bias. Feelings are relevant for certain types of injuries or damages in civil cases. Ambivalent questions should be avoided.

"How did you react?" (ambivalent, might call for facts or feelings)

"What did you do?" (clearly calls for facts)

"How did that make you feel?" (clearly calls for feelings)

When the case calls for subjective evidence, lawyers should also attempt to get objective facts established that support the subjective evidence. For example, in a self-defense case, if the defendant testifies she felt terrified at the time she pulled her gun out of her purse, it is helpful that an eye witness saw the defendant's hands shaking and can describe the frightened way her voice sounded. These are objective facts that support the defendant's testimony about being terrified.

It is not a good idea to repeatedly use the question: "What happened next?". Although there are circumstances that call for it, lawyers sometimes resort to this question as a crutch. This is a bad habit to get into. Repetition is boring, and this generic, all-purpose question doesn't tie the threads of the story together as more focused questions do. More importantly, this question doesn't give the witness much help or direction. Trial lawyers need to develop sophisticated skills, including the ability to ask focused questions without unnecessary leading.

Good lawyers help the witness and the jury navigate smoothly from one topic or timeframe to another with a clear transition. For example, a lawyer might say,

"Ms. Stewart, let's move on to the date of the stock sale. Where were you on that date?"

"Mr. Borden, I want to ask you now about your car. When did you take your car into the shop for servicing?"

Direct examinations can be brief and still be effective and persuasive. Every question should be necessary. Jurors do not always need background. It depends on the case and the witness. Action facts are more interesting than most background facts, so the direct examiner should get to the action as quickly as possible.

Please state your name.

Ms. Rubio, where do you work?

Where is the Midtown Coffee House?

Were you working at the coffee house on the night of October 3rd?

Did some police officers come into the coffee house that night?

How many officers came inside?

What time did they come in?

Describe what happened when the officers came inside.

TELL THE CLIENT'S STORY THROUGH DIRECT EXAMINATION.

Every question should call for an answer that adds something to the client's case. Jurors need to know who the witness is, what the witness knows, and why it is important.

Keep the case interesting and manageable. Be mindful of jurors' limited attention spans. Be wary of getting unnecessary details from a witness which may open the door to harmful cross examination. Keep a check list of all the important facts and any exhibit foundations for witnesses who testify on direct. Check this list before returning to counsel table to make sure all the necessary facts have made it into the record.

Questions should be organized in a manner that makes it easy for the witness and the jury to follow the story. Witnesses usually find it easy to answer questions in chronological sequence. It depends on the witness's role in the story , so lawyers should remain flexible when drafting outlines. There are times when it is effective to begin with an exciting event and return to background details later on in the examination.

The point when a witness is first introduced and the point when a witness nears the finish line are important. It is persuasive to begin and end on strong facts. For example, jurors might learn at the beginning of the witness's direct testimony that the witness saw a man shooting a gun through a car window. Once they realize they are listening to an eye witness, they will anticipate the story details. A strong finish for the direct examination might be the identification of the shooter by the witness in the courtroom. These facts are naturally powerful, and powerful facts are memorable.

Beginning of eye witness examination:

> Mr. Borden, did you see something memorable on the evening of September 13th?
>
>> (I saw a man point a handgun out of a car window and shoot into another car)

End of the same examination, after the witness has testified in detail:

> Mr. Borden, please look around the courtroom. Do you see the man who fired that gun seated in this room today?
>
>> (Yes, that's him at the counsel table, there)

> Please point to the person you have identified and describe an article of clothing he is wearing.
>
>> (He is wearing a blue shirt and a grey sweater)

> Let the record reflect the witness has pointed to the defendant.

If a defendant testifies on her own behalf, it is helpful for her lawyer to finish the examination with a series of related questions which establish the ultimate point. The jurors will notice when a witness is straightforward and unafraid to address the crucial questions in the trial.

Ms. Jones, did you speak to Julian Smith on June 5th?

Did you see Julian at all on June 5th?

Were you at the Franklin Barbecue at any point that evening?

Did you kill Julian Smith?

Did you have anything at all to do with the death of Julian Smith?

Time lines are important in many cases, so it makes sense to organize witness testimony and other evidence with a beginning, middle, and end.

The pace of testimony is important. Direct examinations should be as much like the narrative of a good book as possible. In some cases, the plot is the focus. The story is a thriller. In others, there is heartbreaking drama. In any event, awkwardly phrased or vague questions ruin a good story. Too much repetition ruins a good story. Long or unfamiliar words ruin a good story.

One way to avoid awkward or vague questions when drafting an outline is to work backwards from the answer to the question. What does the witness need to tell the jurors? If it is something helpful or necessary to the case, a focused question or series of simple but focused questions should be effective.

Facts are difficult to weigh in a vacuum. Jurors need to learn something about the witness because they have to consider and weigh what the witness knows. Witnesses are usually introduced with background facts. Simple background questions allow witnesses to introduce themselves to the jurors. Depending on the witness, background includes information such as name, occupation, employer, education, and relationship to the parties. Witnesses are not usually asked to give their home address or other sensitive personal information unless there is a specific need based on the issues in the case.

Background, or accreditation, is more complex for expert witnesses. The rules of evidence require heightened qualifications for witnesses providing opinions in scientific or technical areas.

Sometimes, negative aspects of a witness's background need to be exposed during direct examination for the sake of credibility. If so, it is best to ask those questions somewhere other than the very beginning or very end. The direct examination should begin and end on strong, positive points. The overall impression should be persuasive and helpful to the party calling the witness.

Prosecutors often need to call cooperating co-defendants or informants as witnesses. If the witness is testifying pursuant to a plea agreement, the best practice is to make that known, including details, during the direct examination.

If a witness has given earlier statements which are different from the witness's testimony at trial, it may be helpful to allow the witness to make this known and explain it during the direct examination. It depends on how strong the impeachment material is and how important the witness is in the case.

Good lawyers avoid the temptation to get *all* possible bad information out before the opposing lawyer can cross examine the witness. When a lawyer gets too many bad facts from her own witness during direct, it sends a mixed and confusing message to the jury. It may appear that the lawyer is unprepared for trial, or ambivalent about her own case. Lawyers should begin and end any line of questioning on strong, favorable evidence.

Lawyers should *listen* to their own witnesses during cross examination. If the cross-examiner scores some major points, it may be helpful to ask one or two rehabilitative questions on redirect examination. If the witness's credibility survives cross examination with little or no damage, it may be best to pass on redirect. It should never be mechanical.

It is not necessary to *always* have the last word. Other considerations are important. Some lawyers rehash old territory or call unnecessary attention to bad facts just to get back in front of the jury after the cross examination. There is a simplistic rationale for this: the jurors will remember the last thing they hear. The truth is more sophisticated. Sometimes redirect examination is needed. With other witnesses, it has the overall effect of weakening the impact of the direct examination. Re-hashing direct for the sake of getting the last word lessens the overall impact of an otherwise good witness.

FIVE GOALS FOR DIRECT EXAMINATION.

The witness (not the lawyer) is the one telling the story.
The story is easy to follow.

The jury is interested in the story.

The jury gets each key point.

Collectively, the points meet the party's burden.

PRINCIPLES OF A WELL-CONDUCTED DIRECT EXAMINATION.

The lawyer should not "feed" the witness disputed facts.

The questions should be organized in a way that allows the story to flow.

The questions should call for important information and helpful details.

The lawyer should seek answers that emphasize or echo the themes in the case.

The lawyer should establish every fact necessary to survive a motion for
directed verdict or judgment of acquittal.

Lawyers who are *overly* concerned about drawing leading objections may end up asking too many questions, awkward questions, or questions that frustrate the witness. The guiding principle is that the witness is the person providing the facts which support disputed claims or defenses. When a lawyer is truly leading a witness, the jurors (not just opposing counsel or the judge) will recognize it. The most persuasive witnesses are witnesses who clearly know the facts and need very little help providing them to the jury.

Lawyers who lead their own witnesses will draw objections from a good opponent. The judge may intervene and sustain these objections, adding disruption to the direct. Leading also creates the appearance that a weak, hesitant, or untruthful witness has been coached.

There is not a blanket prohibition against leading questions on direct examination.[6] The issue is whether essential facts are part of the witness's personal knowledge as opposed to the lawyer's wish list. Lawyers should avoid phrasing direct examination questions as statements of essential facts.

Witnesses should be interviewed in a straightforward, engaging manner. One way to do this is to pull part of the witness's last answer into the next question, sort of like sewing the story line together. Some lawyers refer to this as "looping". The concept is important. Lawyers who paint a rich and complete picture through direct examinations end up with a more persuasive case. If the interview is linear and thorough in detail, witnesses will stay on track.

---

6   FRE 611(c); parallel state provisions

Mr. King, I am going to ask you a few more questions about the day of the job interview:

You mentioned that something was wrong. What was wrong?
> (The supervisor smelled like alcohol)

What is the name of the supervisor who smelled like alcohol?
> (Gretchen Blue)

Was there anything else you noticed about Ms. Blue that day besides the smell of alcohol?
> (She was wobbly)

How could you tell Ms. Blue was wobbly?
> (She kept walking back and forth at the window, and she wobbled the whole time)

When you say, "she wobbled the whole time," how long was it?

The case is new to the jurors. The story needs to make sense to someone who is not already familiar with the facts. Lawyers who forget about this may ask too few questions or jump from topic to topic without clear transitions. A good lawyer listens with a juror's ear.

ALLOW JURORS TO USE VISUAL SENSE DURING DIRECT EXAMINATION.

Photographs, charts, and diagrams should be positioned where the jury can clearly see them.[7] If digital evidence is used, the same concepts apply. If there is too much information on the screen, the exhibit is less helpful. Two or three simple slides are better than one complex slide. When the witness has no further need for an exhibit, the witness should be allowed to return to the witness stand.

Lawyers sometimes leave exhibits in front of the jurors as they continue questioning a witness on a different topic. It may be tempting to leave a powerful

---

7   Digital content is subject to objections like any other evidence.

exhibit in front of jurors for as long as possible, but it is also distracting. The exhibit should be removed from the jurors' center of attention. If the witness is moving on to subjects unrelated to the exhibit, jurors may miss valuable information. The direct examiner should not expect jurors to divide their attention between the exhibit and the witness's testimony. The rules allow for admitted evidence to be sent with jurors into the deliberation room, so it is not necessary to leave evidence on view while moving to different subjects.

A good time for lawyers to return to photographs, charts, and tangible evidence is during closing argument. Powerful visual proof is persuasive during closing. It can be used to support arguments. It makes the closing interesting, and the jurors can give it their full attention without missing other information.

Consider using photographs or a diagram with a witness whenever it will help bring the case to life:

Mr. Kennedy, you mentioned the storeroom at the back of the building. (Lawyer has exhibit) Let the record reflect I am showing opposing counsel state's exhibit A. Your Honor, may I approach the witness?

Mr. Kennedy, I am showing you state's exhibit A for identification purposes. Please look at the exhibit.

Do you recognize it?

What is it?

How do you know that exhibit A is the storeroom?

Does exhibit A fairly show what the storeroom looked like on June 5th, 2017?

The state offers exhibit A into evidence as state's exhibit number one. (the exhibit is admitted)

May we show the exhibit to the jury?

May the witness step down?

Mr. Kennedy, using exhibit one, please show us what you first noticed as you entered the storeroom on the morning of June 5th.

Please show us where the ladder is *usually* located.

What is this square object behind the door?

What is the object to the immediate left of the safe?

Is this the desk you were referring to in your testimony?

Is there any part of the desk which is normally kept locked?

Where is that drawer?

Did you notice that drawer on the morning of June 5th?

How did it look?

EMPOWER THE WITNESSES WHO KNOW THE STORY.

When a powerful witness is testifying, a hush falls over the courtroom. Some witnesses are naturally good communicators, and others struggle to tell or describe what they know. Some witnesses care about what happens in the trial. Others are neutral. Some are easier to work with than others.

During discovery and trial preparation, witnesses should be treated with respect and courtesy. A lawyer who is perfunctory, dismissive, or rude to witnesses *before* trial and then attempts to put on a "better face" for direct examination risks a noticeably uncooperative witness.

Good lawyers maximize the benefit of direct examinations by going over questions with the witnesses before the day of trial. Depositions and other important statements or documents should be provided to the witness during pretrial meetings to make sure there are no surprises during trial testimony. Witnesses should also be familiarized with the process of testifying.

It is helpful to take clients or other key witnesses to the courtroom where the testimony will be given. If possible, the witness should become familiar with the place he will be sitting while testifying.

It is also important to give clients and other key witnesses a chance to experience a realistic cross examination. Mock cross exams are part of good trial preparation.

Does the client have a realistic sense of how she will come across on the witness stand? Has her lawyer talked with her about being polite and straightforward? Has her lawyer done everything possible to help her understand the importance of credibility in a jury trial? Has her lawyer prepared her as much as possible to avoid the element of surprise during the trial?

Witnesses sometimes forget details. It is helpful to walk important witnesses through the process of refreshing memory in case this becomes necessary during direct examination. For example:

Officer Graves, was the sliding glass door on the south side of the porch open or closed when you arrived? (witness cannot remember)

Might it refresh your memory about the door if you could look at a copy of your report?

    (showing report to opposing counsel)

Judge, may I approach the witness?

Officer Graves, is this your report?

Please look at the first paragraph on the 2d page and read it to yourself. When you finish reading, please look up.

Is your memory refreshed on that point?

What position was the sliding glass door in when you got to the house?

The officer's report is not an evidence exhibit. It is just being used to refresh his memory on a fact. The rules permit lawyers to show witnesses reports or other items which could reasonably refresh their memory. Some judges ask that these items be marked for identification purposes, and some do not.

Clients and other witnesses need to understand how to present what they know. They need to be mentally prepared. This is important for all aspects of the trial, but especially for direct and cross examination. Has the client been prepared to maintain his composure during cross examination as well as direct? Will he be able to remain calm and stay focused during testimony from adverse witnesses and remarks from opposing counsel?

In the process of preparing for trial, lawyers naturally think of their own responsibilities in the courtroom. It is easy to forget how important it is to help clients and other key witnesses prepare.

Jurors draw clues from the way people *act* and *react*, whether lawyers want them to or not.

MAKE THE WITNESS THE FOCUS OF DIRECT EXAMINATION.

Lawyers should always be aware of the place where jurors are focusing their attention. During the client's case-in-chief, the witnesses and other forms of evidence should be the focal points. Lawyers should never block the jurors' line of vision. During direct examinations, a lawyer should be positioned so that the jurors can easily see the witness. The lawyer and the witness should make eye contact during the interview. If the lawyer appears uninterested in the witness's answers, the jurors may be uninterested as well.

Nothing should be directly between the lawyer and the witness. If possible, the podium should be off to the side. Notes should be left on the podium. It is essential that a lawyer know the case well enough to conduct the direct examination without having her face buried in notes or (worse) a computer. Direct examination outlines should be in bullet-points. Lawyers should *know* what they need from the witness. Lawyers who write out each question in long form may be tempted to read the prepared questions instead of conducting an interesting interview and listening to each answer.

Ideally, the only purpose for notes is to double check before ending the examination and make sure nothing was omitted.

In some jurisdictions, lawyers remain seated at counsel table during witness examinations. In others, the podia may be hard-wired and therefore not movable. Judges sometimes require lawyers to remain at the podium. In any event, eye contact is essential. If the lawyer is not actively engaged in the interview, the jurors are less likely to be alert and fully engaged. It is dangerous to assume that a good closing argument can compensate for a series of poorly done or weak direct examinations.

DEAL INTELLIGENTLY WITH BAD FACTS.

It is sometimes best to "inoculate" a witness by addressing credibility problems during direct. In other instances, it is better to see how the cross examination goes, and, *if necessary*, do some damage control in redirect. It depends on how significant the credibility issue is. If it is very significant, the direct examiner should address it in the most minimal but accurate way possible.

Some lawyers are too anxious when it comes to bad facts. In their quest to de-sensitize the jury by getting the bad facts out early, they end up sending a mixed message. Is the witness credible or not? In the worst-case scenario, a lawyer will go further into bad facts during direct than the cross examiner could have gone without the added "help." A direct examiner who has the witness over-explain credibility or bias problems may open doors that were previously closed to the other side.

Witnesses naturally try to defend their own character. A witness who is anxious to paint himself as a good person may end up opening the door for the cross examiner to use to previously inadmissible bad character evidence in response. Witnesses who try to over-explain negatives end up creating more opportunity for the cross examiner. The jurors also hear the bad facts more than once.

In circumstances where it is important to address bad facts early, it should be done in a straightforward manner, without a lot of window dressing:

Plaintiff's counsel to a witness who made prior contradictory statements:

Mr. Richards, have you said something different about this accident before today?

What did you say about it earlier?

Why did you say that?

What is different about today?

Prosecutor to cooperating co-defendant:

Ms. Fleet, do you have a plea agreement in this case?

When did you enter into the agreement?

What are the terms of the agreement?

What is your responsibility in the agreement?

REDIRECT EXAMINATION.

The client's facts should come through direct examination. Redirect examination has two possible benefits: to mend damage done during cross examination, and to allow the party who called the witness to have the last word. Many lawyers use redirect to the detriment of the client by simply rehashing their direct. If the witness is strong and helpful, it is not necessary to have the last word. The jurors get it. Information that is interesting and helpful the first time around is not made better by repetition. The opposite may occur—it may begin to sound like a script. The jurors may be ready to change the channel.

While listening to cross examination by the opponent, lawyers must quickly decide whether they *need* to fix any damage. They must also assess whether there is an effective question that will work to fix the damage. If the witness has held up well during cross examination, there should be no redirect exam. If there is a good reason to ask the witness something on redirect, the questions should specifically address issues from cross examination. Redirect examination is limited to the scope of cross examination. If redirect questions are leading, it is proper for the cross examiner to object.

When the direct examinations are over, how much has the jury learned, and how much has it helped the client's case? Have the witnesses been presented to their full potential? Have all the claims, elements, or defenses been covered in the client's case-in-chief? Was damage control done to the extent possible without sending a mixed message?

It is important to develop direct examination skills. One way is to practice a direct examination with the actual witness and have a colleague as a "juror." Can the colleague reconstruct the events the witness has described? Can the colleague "see" what happened as if it was captured on someone's cell phone? Is the interview fresh and interesting? Is the lawyer listening to the witness's answers and asking the next logical question? Does the witness come across in a positive and credible way?

Rather than drafting full questions, experienced lawyers organize the witness's story details in simple bullet points. Lawyers should look at their witnesses, and not at their notes, during direct examination. Lawyers who know their case well rarely look at notes. From the outset, it is best to get into the habit of looking at the witness and engaging in a live interview as opposed to reading a list of questions.

CHECKLIST FOR DIRECT EXAMINATION.

Is the witness in the logical place in the case-in-chief?
Does the witness understand what will be asked?
How can this witness be presented to his full potential?
How can bad facts or credibility issues be neutralized or absorbed?
What exhibits belong with this witness's direct examination?
What are the best ways to begin and end the examination?

Use statement form (lead the witness).

Cross on facts, not conclusions.

Make one point per question.

Be precise.

Listen to the answers.

Don't ask for information. Get an admission (a "yes").

Don't rehash the opponent's case (if it doesn't help, don't ask).

Keep the witness out of your lane (it's a one-way street).

Don't ask unless you know the answer (this is not the time for discovery).

Be prepared to impeach.

Ask deadly questions with a professional tone.

Quit while you are ahead.

Each cross-examination point is a contest or battle in the greater war of the trial. Somebody is going to win. The cross examiner may win. The witness may win. The contest is rarely a draw. Lawyers who are highly successful at cross examination follow these rules:

USE STATEMENT FORM.

Cross examination "questions" should be *statements* in question form. The only reason they are in the question category is because the cross examiner is seeking a "yes" after each statement. A good cross examination is a series of statements. If the statements are effective, the witness should be responding with a series of one-word answers: "yes."

Cross examination is *very* different from direct examination. In a good cross examination, leading questions are used for purposes of obtaining an admission of fact (a "yes"), or impeachment. The cross examiner does not want to enable the witness. The cross examiner is not trying to get information from the witness. The cross examiner does not want to add anything to the other side's case.

The form of question has nothing to do with the *tone*. Unlike the exagerrated hostility of witnesses in popular fiction, many witnesses in the real world are cooperative on cross examination. The tone of the examination should be professional but polite. If a lawyer comes off as rude to a likeable witness, the examination may backfire.

CROSS ON FACTS, NOT CONCLUSIONS. DRAW THE CONCLUSIONS AT THE END OF THE TRIAL, IN CLOSING.

Witnesses should be cross examined with facts and not conclusions. An adverse witness will rarely agree with *conclusions* drawn by the cross examiner. The conclusions will flow logically from facts admitted during cross, and the time to draw the conclusions is closing argument. Cross examination points are essentially ammunition to be used in closing.

MAKE ONE POINT PER QUESTION.

On cross examination, the lawyer is seeking a "yes" or a "no." This is only possible if each cross-exam question addresses a single point. Short, simple questions are also easier for jurors to follow. The longer a question becomes, the easier it is for an adverse witness to use the extra information to her advantage. Cluttered cross examination questions often help the wrong side. Witnesses can do less qualifying or explaining when a question is short and to the point. Compound questions are also objectionable, so the opposing party can disrupt a cross examiner who asks compound questions.

WITNESSES CANNOT GET AROUND FACTS. THEY *CAN* GET AROUND ADJECTIVES, ADVERBS, AND SUBJECTIVE IDEAS. BE OBJECTIVE, NOT SUBJECTIVE.

Cross exam questions should be fact-based. They should be objective. *Facts* that are fairly within the witness's knowledge can be admitted or denied. In contrast, questions containing adjectives and other subjective terms allow the witness to give conditional answers or to dodge the point altogether.

BE PRECISE.

Precise cross examination questions are very effective. If a question is fact-based and addresses a single point, precision should come easily. When a lawyer demonstrates precise knowledge of the facts, jurors notice. Exact quotes are better than paraphrasing. Understatements or overstatements allow the witness wiggle room. Ambivalent questions invite ambivalent answers.

Terms that are open to different interpretations should be avoided. An adverse witness naturally resists agreement with the cross examiner. Similarly, subjective questions invite a witness to get past a "yes" or "no" and back to the other side's agenda. Argumentative or rhetorical questions invite the witness to get into a debate. Argumentative cross examination is also objectionable.

Lawyers who struggle during cross examination are often trying to make the witness agree with their closing argument points instead of getting the admissions they need to *support* those points.

Subjective questions (the witness wins):

> You made things pretty difficult for my client at the plant, didn't you?
> (no, I wouldn't say that)

> His schedule was worse than other employees?
> (better in some ways, worse in others)

He wasn't allowed to take vacation?
>   (that's not true)

Same cross examination with objective questions (the lawyer wins):

You were Mr. Caine's supervisor, right?
>   (yes)

You made the shift assignments?
>   (yes)

You assigned Mr. Caine to the midnight shift?
>   (yes)

For three back-to-back cycles?
>   (he never had a problem with that shift)

But it was three back-to-back cycles?
>   (yes)

Mr. Caine requested paid leave in June of 2015?
>   (Yes, he did request it)

You did not approve that leave request, did you?
>   (that's correct, I did not approve it for that month)

You didn't approve it for the next month either, did you?
>   (no, I didn't)

Two other employees had approved leave in June of that year, correct?
>   (yes)

Subjective/ vague questions:

There were dangerous conditions on the road that morning, weren't there?
>   (not for a safe driver)

Most people stayed at home?

> (most people don't have a 6am shift)

Same cross examination with objective questions:

The schools in your neighborhood were closed that day, right?

> (yes)

County Road 24 was closed between your street and the toll bridge, right?

> (yes)

When you got to 1st street, there was a de-icing machine on the road?

> (yes)

There was only one other car along the route, right?

> (yes)

LISTEN TO THE ANSWERS.

Witnesses have a natural tendency to defend themselves during cross examination. Many witnesses try to avoid answering a question by moving to their own agenda or repeating information helpful to the other side. Lawyers must listen carefully when anything other than a "yes" comes from the witness during cross examination. Witnesses sometimes end up volunteering information that is useful to the cross examiner. They sometimes say things that contradict earlier testimony or statements. They may give non-responsive answers.

Lawyers who stay on a preset, rigid list of questions inevitably miss opportunities during cross examination. The only value to a list is to double check it before ending to make sure everything has been covered. Cross examiners should "zero in" on the witness's direct examination testimony. What was left out? What was sugarcoated? Bias and other credibility issues should be exposed.

If the witness fails to answer the question, it has no value for closing. A strong cross examiner wants to get an admission to each point. Fair questions should be answered.

DON'T ASK FOR *INFORMATION.*

Good cross examinations add nothing to the other side's case. The goal is to take *away* from the other side's case. A good cross examination takes credibility away from the other side. Bias is exposed. Defects are exposed. Weaknesses in the case are exposed. Lawyers who ask open-ended questions on cross often help the wrong side. Open-ended questions allow witnesses to continue adding information for their side instead of admitting the cross-examiner's facts.

Open-ended questions also give the appearance that the lawyer doesn't know things and has to ask the other side's witnesses for information.

DON'T REHASH THE DIRECT EXAMINATION.

The only reason to bring a witness's direct testimony into the cross examination is for impeachment. Otherwise, the cross should pull the focus away from the direct and into areas that help the cross-examiner's client.

DON'T ASK UNLESS YOU KNOW THE ANSWER.

It is dangerous to explore unknown territory on cross examination. Cross is not the time for discovery. When a lawyer is winning a series of cross examination points, it is easy to get a false sense of security with the witness. Lawyers who can't resist risky questions on cross examination often get damaging answers. If the cross examiner invites harmful answers by asking risky questions, he is stuck with the answers.

EXAMPLES OF CROSS EXAMINATION.

Plaintiff's cross of defendant's employee (exposing lack of knowledge):

Mr. West, you started working at the bar in November, right?

Three weeks before Ms. Seton got hurt?

You were still in training, right?

Your position was not yet permanent?

You had never worked on a Friday evening before this one?

This was your first Friday shift, right?

You were working on the deck?

Not at the counter?

None of your customers were at the counter?

You weren't serving at the counter?

You don't know who was drinking at the counter?

You were busy, right?

Doing your assigned job?

You weren't watching someone else's customers?

Another example:
(bias facts)

Ms. Jones, you used to work at the defendant's shop?

You started there after graduation?

You worked there full-time until you had your son, right?

You still come in if the defendant is short-handed?

You know someone named Bob Dunn, right?

You and Mr. Dunn are in a relationship?

You have been together for about 3 years?

You have a child together?

Mr. Dunn works for the defendant, doesn't he?

He is the defendant's nephew?

You have an apartment in Geeville, right?

The defendant pays your rent, doesn't he?

He has paid your rent for almost 2 years?

Defense counsel in personal injury case (bias and favorable story facts):

Mr. Rusk, the plaintiff is your roommate?

You have been roommates for two years?

You are friends, too?

You were going to a party the evening of the accident?

Let's return to 7:30pm, the night of the accident:

You are in the front passenger seat, yes?

The plaintiff is driving the car?

It's raining?

You notice the trees blowing from the wind?

There is a flashing red signal at the intersection, right?

There is a nightclub at the intersection?

There is a spotlight on at the nightclub?

The spotlight is crossing the sky?

You have a green light at the intersection?

The plaintiff drives into the intersection?

You see a television crew?

You put your window down as you enter the intersection?

The plaintiff has his window down too, yes?

You wave at the camera crew?

You call out, "over here!", right?

You stick your head out of the window?

The plaintiff stops in the intersection, doesn't he?

He puts his brakes on, right?

Prosecutor's cross examination of defense alibi witness:

You grew up in Windsor, correct?

You still live there?

But you went to school in Geeville?

For high school, right?

You work in Geeville now, don't you?

You have driven between Windsor and Geeville?

On County Road 15?

Several years?

Many times?

To get to school?

To get to work?

To run errands?

To go shopping?

It's about 20 minutes from Windsor to Geeville, isn't it?

Let's talk about the arts festival.

The arts festival was in Windsor, right?

It started at 10am, didn't it?

It didn't start at 9am, did it?
        (holding defense exhibit up)

This picture, defense exhibit 3, is the picture you were discussing during direct, right?

This picture was taken at the pavilion, right?

That's where the auction was, right?

The auction is underway in this picture, isn't it?

The auction began at 11am, right?

Let's talk about your relationship with the Defendant:

You work with the Defendant, don't you?

The two of you have worked together for 10 years?

You play cards together?

You socialize together?

You go to football games together?

Let's go back to January 7th: You were present when the defendant was arrested, right?

Detective Alice Barnes was there, wasn't she?

You went to school with Detective Barnes, didn't you?

You have known Detective Barnes since grade school?

She was at the plant when the defendant was arrested, right?

She was in the break room when you were on your break?

You didn't ask to speak with her, did you?

Instead, you left the building, didn't you?

You didn't wait outside either, did you?

You didn't say anything to her about the Arts Festival?

Plaintiff's cross of defense witness in wrongful termination case ("devil's advocate" cross/ exposing hypocrisy):

Mr. Flood, you are a loyal employee, aren't you?

You want to do what's best for your employer?

You believe in team work?

You are a team player?

You would help a fellow employee, right?

So you offered to help Mr. Glenn, right?

So he didn't need any help?

Let's look at the timeline together. You complained about the inventory on October 2nd?

But the inventory was done in June, right?

You complained about the sales promotion on October 13th?

The sales promotion that happened in early July, right?

Someone or something prevented you from complaining earlier, right?

You were promoted to assistant manager in September, right?

You made these complaints after your promotion, didn't you?

The goal in cross-examination is to discredit and weaken the opponent's case.

During cross examination, the jury should be focused on the cross-examiner as opposed to the witness, and the content of the questions should be favorable to the cross-examiner's client. Good lawyers avoid re-hashing the direct examination. The cross examiner should not help the witness reinforce his direct examination testimony.

CROSS EXAMINATION IS ONE-WAY TRAFFIC. KEEP THE WITNESS
OUT OF THE LANE.

A good cross examiner is on a one-way street. It is a narrow street, intended for the cross examiner only. This means lawyers must develop skill at keeping the witness out of the lane.

Witnesses often try to get back to their own agenda or somehow qualify their answers in ways that support their side. They may ramble on after making a concession. They may attempt to dodge some questions altogether. They may try to soften the question by rephrasing it or asking a different question in response. It is important for the cross examiner to remain steady and keep the jury's attention on the pending point. If the witness succeeds in pulling the lawyer away from the pending question, control is lost.

EXAMPLES OF WITNESS MANAGEMENT.

But the answer to my question is yes?

I'll repeat the question for you.

Let's come back to the actual question.

So that's a yes, correct?

Ms. X, you are somehow missing the question. Here it is again:

It's a simple question. Let's try again:

Some lawyers try to lecture witnesses before they begin the cross examination. It may sound like a mini procedure quiz. For example, they *instruct* the witness *in advance* to give only "yes" or "no" answers. This is a poor practice. It is objectionable, because the judge (not the lawyer) has authority over trial procedure. The questions have not yet been asked, so neither the witness nor the opposing lawyer know whether the questions can be fairly answered with a "yes" or "no." The bigger issue is juror reaction. Jurors are apt to see this as an attempt by the lawyer to bully the witness, or a signal that the lawyer is afraid of what the witness may say. Lawyers who lecture witnesses also come off as arrogant.

Instead of ineffective shortcuts, good lawyers control witnesses during cross examination by asking leading, single-point, non-argumentative questions.

The witness's knowledge and position in the case should be thoroughly explored before deciding what to cover in cross-examination. A good cross examination outline is cross-referenced to discovery materials that can be used for impeachment. It is important to *listen carefully to the direct examination* during trial and be prepared to *adapt* the cross accordingly. Witnesses often volunteer information that leads to new avenues of impeachment. Sloppy answers may open doors that were previously closed. Other points can be crossed off the outline in cases where anticipated direct examination testimony wasn't given.

AREAS TO CONSIDER WHEN PREPARING FOR CROSS EXAMINATION.

What was intentionally left out of the direct examination?

What helpful facts must this witness admit?[8]

How can this witness's credibility be attacked?

What bias or motive does this witness have, and how should it be exposed?

The cross-examiner should *only* ask questions that help the client's case. Some cross-examinations may be brief. It is better to be brief than to allow answers which help the opponent.

---

8   Lawyers must be mindful of the scope of cross-examination (any area fairly raised in direct examination and credibility/bias/motive facts). FRE 611(b) Scope is broad, but the judge may limit inquiry that covers an entirely different topic. Judges have discretion to permit inquiry into matters outside the scope of direct. They may also require the cross examiner to call the witness in her own case for those matters.

IMPEACHMENT.

Witnesses can be impeached in many ways. Broadly, impeachment is anything that damages the impact of the witness's direct examination. Most (not all) impeachment takes place during cross examination. Impeachment includes:

Prior inconsistent statements
Selective memory (calling attention to it)
Bias or motive to say certain things
Bias or motive to testify for a certain party
Incentives to testify for a certain party
Proof of untruthful character (methods vary by jurisdiction)

Impeachment material is ammunition. It is important to let jurors know when witnesses have changed their testimony or had selective memory lapses. Lawyers should have statements, depositions, and other documents readily available when cross examining a witness. Pages should be tabbed for quick reference. If jurors must wait for the impeachment, the value and impact are lessened.

In limited circumstances, it may be best to forego impeachment. Some witnesses are helpful to both sides and may even be more sympathetic to the cross-examiner's side. On cross-examination, this type of witness is not adverse in the way most witnesses are. Lawyers should avoid the attacking the *truthfulness* of a witness who is essentially a favorable witness, particularly if damaging aspects of the witness's testimony can be handled in a less adversarial way (faulty memory, poor ability to observe, confusion).

Bias comes in many forms. Motives and incentives for witnesses are powerful impeachment material. Bias can be benign or sinister. It can be anywhere in between. Jurors can understand and be influenced by all kinds of bias evidence. It is universally understood. Depending on the facts of the case and the people involved, key witnesses may be biased. The relevance obviously depends on the case.

EXAMPLES OF BIAS.

Witness is family member of the defendant

Witness is a friend of the plaintiff

Witness is an employee of the victim

Witness goes to church with victim

Witness had the same negative experience as the defendant

Witness had the same traumatic event as the victim

Witness is a law enforcement officer

Witness has a racial prejudice

Prosecution witness has a plea agreement

Prosecution witness has pending charges

Prosecution witness is on probation

Witness has negative feelings toward same-sex couples/consuming alcoholic beverages/members of a certain ethnic or religious background/authority figures or law enforcement

This type of evidence is discovered in thorough, full-circle investigation and trial preparation. Lawyers should not underestimate the value of bias evidence in cross examination.

PRIOR INCONSISTENT STATEMENTS SHOULD BE EXPOSED.

Jurors need to know when a witness has changed course. If the trial testimony contradicts earlier statements, there is usually an important reason. The first obvious issue is whether the witness is untruthful. Prior statements that differ in a trivial way should be let alone. Cross examiners who attempt to impeach a witness with a prior statement that means essentially the same thing the witness said in trial come across as petty.

There is a strategic difference between setting up impeachment and setting up refreshment of memory. Lawyers usually refresh memory with sympathetic witnesses (direct examination). Adversarial witnesses should be impeached. Rather than ask a witness whether he *remembers* making a statement, the witness should simply be confronted with the statement.

For example, assume Mr. Volt, a prosecution witness, insists at trial that he saw the Defendant, Howard Denny, throw a gun out of a moving car. He is now under cross examination:

Mr. Volt, you gave a deposition in this case on May 5th, didn't you?

(Setting up impeachment)

Mr. Mason from the State Attorney's Office was present?

Ms. Goldman from our firm was present?

You were at Nobles Court Reporting?

Downtown?

You were placed under oath for the deposition, weren't you?

You swore to tell the truth?

You answered questions about what you saw that night, correct?

You had an opportunity to read your deposition afterwards, correct?

I am now referring to page 6, lines 4 and 5 of your May 5th deposition.

You were asked, "Who threw the gun out of the car?", and your answer was, "Brittany threw it out the window".

That was your answer, correct?

EXAMPLES OF IMPEACHMENT BY PRIOR INCONSISTENT STATEMENT.

> (Defense witness in premises liability case has testified during direct examination that the back stairs were well lit, and she was comfortable using them)

Ms. Douglas, are you sure the stairs were well -lit?

And you felt comfortable using them?

In 2016?

You know a person named Marjorie King, correct?

Ms. King was your co-worker in 2016?

She parked her car in the same lot where you parked yours?

This lot was accessible by the back stairs?

You and Ms. King worked the same shift, yes?

You got off work at the same time?

Ms. Douglas, you talked to Ms. King about those stairs, didn't you?

You spoke to Ms. King 2 days after Callie Dowd was injured, didn't you?

You and Ms. King went running together 2 days after the fall, right?

You told Ms. King you were surprised there weren't *more* people injured, didn't you?

You told Ms. King you were afraid to go down the stairs, didn't you?

You told her you were going to start parking out on the street instead of the employee's lot?

In the above example, plaintiff's counsel should be prepared to call Marjorie King as an impeachment witness if Douglas denies the prior inconsistent statements.

There is a battle of wits involved in cross examination, particularly with a sophisticated witness. Good lawyers avoid falling into argument with a witness, asking for help from the judge, making editorial comments, bullying the witness, making concessions, or anything else that allows the witness to win the question. Jurors notice who wins.

Pace is important in cross-examination, as in direct examination, even though the goals are different. The pace must be up-tempo enough to keep the jurors interested. Rather than pausing frequently or between every question, lawyers should pause or check over notes at a logical breaking point.

A proper tone for cross examination is professional but firm. Yelling, bullying, or sarcasm cast a lawyer in a negative light. If someone looks mean or arrogant in front of the jurors, it is preferably the witness and not the lawyer. Lawyers who lose control of their professional demeanor are effectively telling the jurors that they have lost control over the case.

When the cross-examination is over, has the witness been effectively discredited?

MORE EXAMPLES.

Cross exam of prosecution witness in trial for extortion:

Ms. Ray, you answered the door that afternoon, right?

There was only one person at the door?

A man?

That man had a distinct voice, didn't he?

That was the same voice you heard on the phone the night before, yes?

This man, seated over here at the table, was not the man who came to your home, correct?

The only person who has ever asked you about your son's computer is the man who came to your home January 5th, correct?

The only person who has ever asked you for money in exchange for your son's computer is the man who came to your home January 5th?

Cross exam of prosecution witness who is a cooperating defendant:

Mr. Raft, let's return to the night you were arrested.

You were arrested as soon as you handed the pill bottle to the man you knew as "John", correct?

That's the moment you learned "John" was a police officer, yes?

You were handcuffed then, right?

And taken outside the Bar?

To a patrol car, right?

You were placed in the back of the car?

As you were being placed in the car, you told the officers you didn't know what was in the pill bottle, didn't you?

"I don't know what this stuff is"?

Your words, right?

You asked the officers if you were going to go to jail?

And they told you that you were going to jail, didn't they?

That's when you said you wanted to "turn state's evidence?"

Those were your words, correct?

You sat in the back of the patrol car for about half an hour, right?

While the officers talked outside?

They came back to the car at some point?

And you asked to make a statement?

Let's review the statement you made that night:

You said you got the pills from a man in Jacksonville?

Not Gainesville?

The man's name was Ike?

You didn't say the man's name was Edward, did you?

You met "Ike" at a garage?

On Union Street?

You told the officers you didn't know his last name?

You also said you thought the pills were fake?

They took you to jail then, right?

You were in jail for nine days?

Then you asked to meet with Detective Smith?

You contacted Detective Smith, right?

Not the other way around?

He came to see you on February 9th?

You told Detective Smith you knew the pills were "real," right?

You told him you got the pills in Gainesville?

From a co-worker's brother?

You said you bought the pills at the brother's house, right?

You said you could go back and buy some more pills there, right?

Edward Davis is not your co-worker's brother, is he?

When the officers checked you out of jail, you couldn't tell them where Edward Davis lived, could you?

You couldn't take them to his house, could you?

Cross exam of cooperating defendant with plea bargain:

Let's talk about your plea deal.

You were arrested for sale of a controlled substance, correct?

You could receive up to fifteen years for that offense?

In prison?

With your deal, you will only enter a plea to attempted possession?

That is a misdemeanor offense, isn't it?

The most you could get with your deal is 11 months and 29 days, right?

You can't go to prison?

You hope to get probation, right?

You are not in jail now, are you?

Cross of plaintiff in a personal injury case:

Ms. Krebs, you worked at the Dobson Gallery before the accident?

As a receptionist?

You worked twenty to thirty hours a week?

Your hours varied, right?

Depending on gallery events?

You went back to work after the accident, yes?

Your first day back was May 3rd, 2017?

You worked 23 hours that week, correct?

You worked 27 hours in the following week?

Then you quit?

You gave one week's notice?

You told Mr. Dobson you weren't getting enough hours, didn't you?

You wanted 40 hours a week, yes?

You never complained to him about back pain, did you?

You didn't mention any discomfort of any kind?

Cross of eye witness to a fight:

Mr. Taylor, you were inside the hotel for dinner, correct?

Your table was along the wall?

Not along the window?

When you got outside, you saw 2 people on the ground?

They were already on the ground?

You don't know how they got there?

You don't know who hit the ground first?

You don't know the man with the red hair?

You don't know the man with the grey suit?

QUIT WHILE YOU ARE AHEAD.

All experienced trial lawyers know about the dreaded "one question too many." They also know about the occasional and dangerous open-ended cross examination question. Once the witness has admitted all the facts needed for closing argument, it is wise to stop. The temptation to keep scoring points may lead to a reversal in fortunes.

Anecdotally, most lawyers can think of times when an open-ended cross examination question or a "wild card" question was asked, and the answer was helpful. This is not surprising, given the infinite variety of witnesses, issues, cases, and pure chance. Sometimes risks pay off, but they are still risks. Risk should always be weighed against the need for caution, because a client's interests are at stake.

What is this item?

How do we know what it is?

Who has personal knowledge of what it is?

How is the item important in the case?

What steps are needed to get it admitted?

Foundations for evidence come from people with knowledge. All types of evidence need a foundation of reliability. For eye witness testimony, the foundation is implicit. Once witnesses take the stand and begin to describe their background and their experiences at certain places and times, it is apparent they were using their senses at those places and times. It is apparent that they can communicate in the courtroom and relate what they saw. They are also under an oath or affirmation to be truthful.

Most evidence is in the form of live testimony. The foundation for live testimony is laid by demonstrating the witness's competence and personal knowledge of facts. [9] Foundation and relevance together form a *context* for the evidence. Foundations are necessary for two reasons: First, lawyers must persuade the judge to allow the evidence. Second, foundations help jurors understand and evaluate different types of evidence. For example:

The more we know about a witness, the easier it is to evaluate what they say.

The more history we have about an object, the easier it is to determine its authenticity and importance in the case.

---

9   Competence of witnesses is elemental, and often overlooked. Authenticity of items is another layer of foundation which is built upon the first– the competence of the testifying witness. For a detailed analysis of foundations, see Edward J. Imwinkelried, *Evidentiary Foundations*, (10th Ed. 2014).

Setting the scene, adding historical facts, and adding real and demonstrative evidence make it easier for jurors to decide issues.

Objects, pictures, diagrams, documents, records, and recordings usually need a person to help establish their authenticity. This is not always the case. Some evidence is self-authenticating by statute or rule. Some evidence can be authenticated with a "shortcut" unless the opposing party makes a showing of unreliability. For example, some types of electronically generated and stored information can be authenticated with an affidavit of a qualified person.

Foundations for physical evidence come from a witness's historical knowledge of an object. The foundation includes information about the witness *and* the object. In most jurisdictions, there are some items deemed by statute to be self-authenticating. A common example is a document under seal by the clerk of court. Authentication is just the first step for admissibility. Admissibility calls for authentication, relevance, and fairness. Lawyers must consider foundation as a multi-layered process.

The foundation for expert witnesses is a heightened or magnified version of the foundation for other witnesses. Expert witnesses have the privilege of giving opinions in areas where other witnesses would be confined to personally known, historical facts.

Properly qualified experts are permitted to give opinions on critical issues, including ultimate issues, when their opinions will assist the jurors. For this reason, an expert's credentials and familiarity with the facts and issues in the case are subjected to scrutiny. Is the expert qualified in her field? Is her opinion within the scope of her expertise? Does she have sufficient knowledge of the facts to give a reliable opinion? Has she used validated, reliable methodology in arriving at her opinion? Will her opinion assist the jurors in deciding an issue in the case?

REAL AND DEMONSTRATIVE EVIDENCE.

Jurors need to see evidence. In some cases, they need to handle evidence. Unlike good fiction, which invites readers to use their imaginations, jurors need *proof* of what happened at a real place and time.

Lawyers should think broadly about potential exhibits. Foundation witnesses should be thoroughly familiar with exhibits before the trial. All exhibits and visual aids should be easy to see and easy to understand.

Words alone are rarely enough to prove a case. Lawyers must know how to successfully offer other forms of evidence. There is no limit to the things which might be important in a trial. Guns, drugs, medical records, soil samples, correspondence, invoices, diagrams, pictures, recordings, latent fingerprint lifts, cast shoeprint impressions, e-mails, text messages, and social media pages are just a few examples of things which are placed before jurors in courtrooms across the country.

Before jurors can consider these things, two tests must be met: authentication and relevance. These tests form a threshold for all types of evidence. Lawyers must determine which witness or witnesses are necessary to authenticate items of evidentiary value. Sometimes the relevance is apparent. In other cases, the same witness or different witnesses must establish relevance.

Who has the knowledge needed to connect the evidence to the story?

Physical evidence is powerful. Consider a gun discovered in the jacket pocket of a robbery suspect, or a support cable that has snapped on a bridge. Another example would be the house keys of a murder victim. What if these keys were found in the office of a suspect?

Correspondence and other recorded information is also powerful in trial. Casual writing and conversations between people often "connect the dots" for jurors. E-mails or text messages may show intent, plan, knowledge, or motive in a murder case. Letters or greeting cards help establish the nature of relationships between people. Phone records are often used to prove the timing or extent of communications between specific people. Cell tower information is important as a means of demonstrating the physical area where a call was placed or received. Corporate records may be of great value in a products liability case. Medical records may be essential in bringing or defending a malpractice case.

Images are powerful. Consider the value of a video showing an arson suspect purchasing accelerants shortly before a fire. Suppose a witness testifies that his neighbor stole his class ring in August, but pictures he has posted on social media show he was still wearing his "stolen" ring in December? Suppose a police officer claims he stopped a car for defective brake lights, but the dash camera in the officer's patrol car shows the brake lights on the car were functioning properly?

These are examples of evidence that does not come directly from the mouth of witnesses. Non-testimonial evidence has special appeal for jurors. They can accept a gun or picture at face value. They can compare correspondence or records to things witnesses are saying in the courtroom. They can read, watch, and handle things that existed prior to the time a court case was born. They can weigh these things without having to factor in motives or truthfulness.

Here are some things to consider when preparing to offer physical (real) evidence:

Who has personal knowledge of the item?
Who took possession of it when it became relevant to the case?
Who can identify the item as being the same one relevant to the case?
Who has knowledge of where it has been since it became relevant to this case?[10]
Who can state that the trial-date condition is substantially the same as the condition on the date the item became relevant?

The best foundation witness is not always a primary or eye witnesses. For example, if a gun is relevant in a robbery case, the officer who collected the gun should be called and questioned for purposes offering the gun into evidence. This officer may have little or no other involvement in the case, but he is still the one capable of authenticating the gun. He knows where the gun was found. He noted the maker, the model, and the serial number of the gun in his report. He secured the gun and placed it in an evidence locker. If there are any other unique characteristics about the gun, he observed them first hand at the time he collected the gun. He is the proper foundation witness because of this knowledge.

The robbery victim may have gotten a mere glimpse of the gun. The victim will not have enough knowledge to authenticate the gun at trial.

Sometimes scientific or technical analysis has been performed on an item of evidence by an expert witness. This means that more than one witness may discuss the item during the trial.

What does the jury need to know about a certain item? How does the item prove or disprove an issue in the case? Is this white powdery substance cocaine? Is there a toxic chemical in this soil sample? Are the defendant's fingerprints on this piece of paper? Is the victim's DNA in the defendant's car?

Judges sometimes admit items into evidence before the last step is taken. For example, a judge might allow a baggie of white powder found in the defendant's

---

10   This is important if there is an issue of tampering or contamination of samples, and less significant if a witness can plainly authenticate an item. FRE 901; In Florida, §90. 901(3) F.S.; Bush v. Florida, 543 So. 2d 283 (Fla. App. 2d Dist. 1989); Dodd v. Florida, 537 So. 2d. 626 (Fla. App. 3d Dist. 1988).

home into evidence conditionally, pending testimony by a qualified chemist that the powdery substance is cocaine. In another jurisdiction, the powder might not be formally admitted into evidence until the chemist has testified.

In some circumstances, lawyers need to move the court for a jury view of relevant locations, structures, or evidence which is too big to bring into the courtroom.

IDENTIFYING EVIDENCE FOR THE RECORD.

Testimony can be transcribed. Tangible items must be identified by some other means in the record. For this reason, lawyers have items marked for identification purposes. If the item is admitted into evidence, it receives an evidence letter or number as well. A deputy clerk is usually the one who "follows" the evidence in the trial and applies evidence labels. The exact way evidence is marked varies from jurisdiction to jurisdiction. For purposes of appeal, any item referenced in the trial should be identifiable.

Most judges have items marked (labeled) by the court clerk as soon as they are admitted. Other judges allow lawyers to continue with witness examinations and have their items marked during breaks between witnesses or recesses. Items that have been formally admitted as trial evidence generally remain in the custody of the clerk when not in use during the trial.

FOUNDATION CHECKLIST.

If item was not marked for identification prior to trial, have it marked by deputy clerk.
Show item to opposing counsel.
Ask permission to approach the witness (with item inside evidence bag or otherwise not displayed to jurors)
Ask questions to establish authenticity:

Mr. Duke, I am showing you state's exhibit A for identification. Please look in the bag and tell us whether you recognize exhibit A.

(Yes, I recognize it)

What is exhibit A?

(These are my keys, on my key chain)

How do you know exhibit A is your set of keys?

(I recognize my house and office keys and the key to my riding mower. Also, I recognize this old key chain my wife gave me)

Are your keys in substantially the same condition as they were on June 5, 2013, the date you testified to earlier?

(Yes)

Your Honor, we offer state exhibit A into evidence as state's number one.

(Exhibit is admitted without objection)

Your Honor, may we show exhibit one to the Jury?

(Yes, you may) (afterwards, keys are tagged with trial evidence label by clerk)

SAMPLE OF FOUNDATION FOR A PICTURE.

(Showing opposing counsel the picture, then approaching the witness)

Ms. Dover, I am showing you plaintiff's exhibit C for identification purposes. Please look at exhibit C and state whether you recognize it.

What does exhibit C show?

How do you recognize this as the lobby of the Blue Skye Resort?

Is exhibit C a fair representation of the way the hotel lobby appeared on January 7, 2016?

We offer exhibit C into evidence as plaintiff's number three.

(picture admitted without objection) (back of picture labeled by clerk)

Your Honor, may we show exhibit three to the jurors?
(using exact enlarged copy on easel)

Sample foundation for image posted on social media:
(Showing opposing counsel printout of image posted on a social media website)

May I approach the witness?

Ms. Slade, I am showing you plaintiff's exhibit B for identification. Please look at exhibit B for us.

Do you recognize exhibit B?

What is exhibit B?

How do you know exhibit B is a picture from the graduation party?

Other than the fact that you are in the picture, are there other ways you know this image is from the graduation party?

Is exhibit B one of the images you were referring to earlier in your testimony?

Does exhibit B fairly show the way your group's table looked on May 19th, 2016?

We offer plaintiff's exhibit B into evidence as plaintiff's exhibit number two.
(admitted without objection) (marked by clerk)

May we publish plaintiff's exhibit two?
(published by slide up on screen)

Ms. Slade, please identify the people seated at your table in exhibit number two.

Sample of foundation for business record:

Mr. Gonzalez, where are you employed?

How long have you worked at the University Athletic Association?

What is your position there?

As part of your job, do you assist in keeping records?

What type of records do you keep?

What is a swim permit?

When is a swim permit issued?

Who prepares the permit?

Who provides the information that is recorded on the permit?

Does the Athletic Association keep a record of swim permits?

How are the records stored?

How long are these records kept?

Are swim permit records kept in the ordinary course of business at the Athletic Association?
>   (showing exhibit to opposing counsel)

Let the record reflect I am showing opposing counsel defense exhibit D. May I approach the witness?
>   (approaching witness)

Mr. Gonzalez, I am showing you defense exhibit D for identification purposes. Please look at exhibit D.

Do you recognize exhibit D?

What is it?

How is it that you recognize exhibit D as a swim permit from the Athletic Association?

Have you seen exhibit D before today?

When did you last see this exhibit?

Has the exhibit been altered in any manner since you brought it to our office?

Your Honor, we offer exhibit D into evidence as defense exhibit 4.
    (admitted without objection) (back of permit labeled by clerk)

May we publish the exhibit on the screen, your honor?

Sample of foundation for evidence collected by law enforcement:

Officer Shelly, please describe the item you found in the space between the front seats.
    (I found a small, clear plastic baggie, about 3 inches by 3 inches, containing 5 pieces of a white, chalky substance)

What did you do with this item?
    (I placed it in a larger plastic baggie and sealed that baggie. I then placed a label on the outer baggie with the date, my initials, and the case report number)

After it was labeled, what did you do with it?
    (I placed it in an evidence locker in the trunk of my patrol car. At the end of my shift, I removed it from the evidence locker in my trunk and placed it in a secure locker in our evidence room at the station)

Who has access to the evidence locker at the station?

The officer securing the evidence and the evidence custodian.

Have you seen it since then?

(Yes, I looked at it before court this morning, here in the courthouse)

Did you bring the baggie to the courthouse, or did someone else bring it?
(Our evidence custodian brought it to court)

(Lawyer showing item to opposing counsel) (item inside folder) Let the record reflect I am showing defense counsel state's exhibit B for identification purposes. May I approach the witness?

Officer Shelly, I am showing you state's exhibit B for identification. Please look inside this folder and tell us whether you recognize the exhibit.
(Yes)

How do you recognize it?
(It has my initials, date June 11th, and the case report number, and it is packaged as I mentioned earlier)

What is state's exhibit B?
(The baggie containing small white objects we found in between the seats of the defendant's car)

Is the baggie in substantially the same condition as it was when you placed it in your trunk?
(Yes, it is the same except for markings from the state crime laboratory)

Can you identify those differences?
(Yes, they have re-sealed the top of the outer baggie with a blue tape that has state crime lab identification. Also, underneath my label, there is a blue crime lab label indicating date received/ date returned, analyst's initials, and a lab number)

Your Honor, we offer exhibit B into evidence as state's number two.
(item is admitted) (outer baggie labeled by clerk)

May we show the exhibit two to the jurors?

In the above example, the next logical witness for the prosecution would be the analyst who tested the substance. If an issue of tampering is raised by the defense, the evidence custodian might also be called to testify.

Lawyers admitting evidence must be prepared to satisfy both the judge and the jury that the evidence is authentic and reliable. If the judge is not persuaded, the evidence will never get to the jurors. If it does get to the jurors, there may still be concerns about reliability. Any concerns the jurors have may work against the side offering the evidence.

CONTROVERSIAL EVIDENCE.

Evidence is subject to challenge by the opponent if it is highly emotionally charged or of a disturbing nature. In these cases, the best time to address admissibility is pretrial, when there is still time for a fallback position. The side offering the challenged evidence should be prepared to explain its relevance. Judges may limit the size or number of disturbing images. Lawyers may be required to offer some images in black-and-white rather than graphic color. Some evidence may be excluded altogether if there is other less shocking or disturbing evidence available to prove the same facts.

EVIDENCE CHECKLIST.

Subpoena for necessary foundation witnesses
Is the evidence self-authenticating? (FRE 902)
Is an evidence custodian needed? (chain of custody at issue)
Exact enlargements or digital slides for juror viewing
Witness preparation
(If necessary) bullet-point outline of foundation questions
Caselaw

EXPERT WITNESSES

EXPERT OPINIONS ARE NECESSARY IN SOME CASES.
LAWYERS MUST KNOW THE THRESHOLD REQUIREMENTS FOR
EXPERT TESTIMONY.
LAWYERS MUST UNDERSTAND AN EXPERT'S FIELD, THE
UNDERLYING FACTS, AND THE OPINION WELL ENOUGH TO
HANDLE DIRECT OR CROSS EXAMINATION INTELLIGENTLY.

If the lawyer doesn't get it, they jury probably won't get it either.

Federal and state rules permit experts to give testimony in areas beyond the knowledge of lay witnesses.[11] The rules permit properly qualified experts to give *opinions,* so the foundation for their testimony is more complex than that for lay witnesses. Lay witnesses are generally limited to facts. When preparing to offer or challenge expert testimony, lawyers should consider these factors:

What education, training, knowledge, experience, or skill does the witness have beyond that of an average person? In other words, does the witness have expertise that will assist the jury in understanding the evidence or deciding the issues in the case?

What is the area and scope of expertise of the witness?

Do the jurors *need* expert testimony to understand the evidence or decide an issue in the case?

---

11   FRE 701-706; parallel state rules.

Does the expert have sufficient knowledge of the case to assist the jurors?

Is the expert capable of testifying in a manner that will assist the jurors in deciding the case?

Will the expert be permitted to offer an opinion under the law of the jurisdiction?

Generally, opinions grounded in science must be shown to be based on reliable methodology.

Expert testimony is necessary in many cases. DNA evidence may be the only direct link between the defendant and a homicide victim. An engineer's opinion may be the only basis jurors have to decide whether a design defect was the legal cause of the plaintiff's severe injuries. A medical expert's opinion on causation may be the only thing to get the plaintiff's case past a motion for directed verdict. An entomologist's opinion may establish doubt as to when a body was placed in a certain location.

Lawyers must know how to properly qualify their experts and present expert testimony in a persuasive manner. The testimony must be understandable and credible to be persuasive. Before an expert is permitted to give her opinion, the judge must be satisfied that the opinion is admissible based on the law of the jurisdiction as well as underlying principles of fairness. Because of the expense involved in presenting expert witnesses, good lawyers resolve preliminary questions about admissibility ahead of trial.

Expert testimony can be challenging. Most lawyers are not also molecular biologists, neurologists, metallurgists, orthopedic surgeons, or any other sort of expert. A good lawyer overcomes the challenge of expert testimony by making sure he understands the issue, the opinion, and the basis of the opinion well enough to handle it in trial. Many lawyers become knowledgeable in a scientific or medical field because of the high number of cases they handle in the same area.

Like other witnesses, an expert witness should be doing most of the talking during direct examination. The difference is, instead of telling *what* happened, experts are usually explaining *why*. Rather than giving facts, experts usually rely on a *given* set of facts. Sometimes the facts are in dispute. In these situations, hypothetical questions are sometimes used.

Experts educate jurors and explain evidence in a way that lay witnesses do not, so it is common for their answers to be longer. There may be more "moving parts" to the expert's testimony.

It is usually best to present expert testimony after the jurors have heard the key fact witnesses. If the expert relied in part on records and other admissible documents, they should be offered prior to the expert's opinion.

SAMPLE OUTLINE FOR DIRECT OF MENTAL HEALTH EXPERT (INSANITY DEFENSE).

Name
Area of Practice
How long practiced
Education-- Degrees
Other background
(residency)
(fellowships)
Prior work in the profession
Current Practice—position
Clinical Experience
Teaching experience
Publications
Professional Associations
Licensed (where)
Board Certified?
What is board certification?
Difference between psychiatrist and psychologist
Testified in court before -- as expert witness—
    In what areas/subjects
    How many times?

What types of cases?
For plaintiff, defense, or both?
How many criminal cases?
For state, defense, or both?
Consultation is what percentage of your work?

Testimony is what percentage of your work?

What percentage is in clinical practice?

Teaching?

Have you been paid for your work in this case?

How much?

Are you paid for a specific opinion?

How do you bill for your work? (based on hours, not results)

How did you become involved in this case?

How do you go about forensic assessment?

How did you go about your work in this case?

What kind of information/materials did you have available?

How do you obtain the information you need for your work?

How did you obtain information in this case?

Are you prepared to give an opinion within a reasonable degree of psychiatric certainty as to Ms. J's ability to understand what she was doing/appreciate the nature of her actions 6/5/2013?

What is your opinion?

Please explain

How did you arrive at your opinion?

Are you prepared to give an opinion within a reasonable degree of psychiatric certainty as to Ms. J's ability to understand the wrongfulness of her actions 6/5/2013?

Please explain

What is paranoid schizophrenia

Characteristics

Symptoms

(Have witness step down for use of board or visual aid if helpful)

Relate to history of Ms. J

Go to time of shooting—explain Johnson's *behavior* in terms of her mental illness

Discuss facts/circumstances which support the opinion

Ask witness to address facts which might appear to lead to contrary result

As to each, have witness explain why opinion does not change

End on point regarding her inability to understand difference between right and wrong

or to appreciate nature and consequences of her actions.

Experts make mistakes

You make mistakes

You have made mistakes in your work as an expert

Psychiatry is not an exact science

Experts can differ

A person can be mentally ill and still understand what she is doing

A person can be mentally ill and still understand it is wrong to kill someone

Your opinion must be based on facts

If you have the wrong facts, your opinion is compromised

If you have incomplete facts, your opinion is compromised

Only interviewed defendant in person (no other live interviews)

Only spoke with family members of defendant on phone

SAMPLE DIRECT EXAMINATION OF A NEUROLOGIST.

Good morning. Please introduce yourself.

Dr. Wright, what is your field of practice?

What is neurology?

What does a neurologist do?

What types of patients do you have?

Let's talk some about your background. What degrees do you hold?

Beginning with your undergraduate education, where did obtain your degrees?

Did you do one or more internships as part of your education?

Where were those done?

What areas of medicine were they in?

Did you do a residency?

What is a residency?

After completing your residency, what did you do?

Are you licensed to practice medicine?

What licenses do you hold?

Are you board certified in any area?

In what area or areas?

What is board certification?

Do you currently have a clinical practice?

Do you also do forensic work?

What is the difference between clinical and forensic neurology?

Have you published books or articles in the field of neurology?

Has you work been peer reviewed?

Please explain briefly.

Have you been involved in research in your field?

What types of research have you done?

Do you belong to any professional associations?

What are those?

Do you teach in the field of neurology?

Where have you taught?

Dr. Wright, have you testified in court in your capacity as a neurologist?

How many times have you testified in court as an expert?

Where have you testified?

What types of cases have you testified in?

Have you testified for the prosecution in criminal cases?

Have you testified for the defense?

Have you also testified in civil cases?

For plaintiffs?

For the defense, in civil cases, as well?

Do you testify in every case you work on, or just some cases?

Have you been asked to evaluate professional athletes?

Is that part of your practice?

Have you evaluated NFL players?

Have you evaluated boxers?

Dr. Wright, let's turn our attention to your work in this case. How did you get involved in this case?

What is it that we asked you to do in this case?

What type of information did you receive about the case?

What were your sources of information?

Did you ask for certain types of information in addition to what you were initially provided?

What additional information did you request?

Who did you ask?

Were you able to obtain that information?

We will return to some of that information later this morning. Doctor, is there a process you use when you are going about a diagnosis in a case like this?

What is differential diagnosis?

Can you give us some examples of possible explanations that you considered in Mr. Taylor's case?

In addition to the symptoms and the historical information you studied, did you also perform a clinical examination?

Please explain how you go about a clinical examination.

Were you able to form an opinion in this case?

Is your opinion within a reasonable degree of medical probability or certainty?

What is your opinion?

Please explain what chronic traumatic encephalopathy is.

Is the shorthand term "CTE" commonly used for chronic traumatic encephalopathy?

Doctor, please explain how you went about your diagnosis.

How did you go about ruling out other things we discussed earlier, such as Alzheimer's disease, or a birth injury?

Is there a relationship between CTE and behavior?

How do we know about this relationship?

What is the relationship between CTE and behavior?

As a neurologist, do you use PET scans?

What is a PET scan?

Was a PET scan done in Mr. Taylor's case?

When was it done?

Who ran it?

Have you reviewed Mr. Taylor's PET scan?

As it relates to your opinions, can you explain the significance of what you see in Mr. Taylor's PET scan?
> (retrieving slides used with previous medical witness)

SAMPLE DIRECT EXAMINATION OF EXPERT IN THE AREA OF FIRE ORIGIN AND CAUSE/ARSON.

> (after background, credentials, and history as expert witness)

Captain Barton, were you asked by your department to go to a residence in Geeville in the early morning hours of August 3, 2017?

Where did you go?

What were you asked to do at that address?

What is an "origin and cause" investigation?

Please describe what you saw when you got to 117 Jump Street.

Did you meet with anyone when you arrived?

What was the purpose of the meeting?

At some point, did you go around to the back of the house?

What did you observe at the back of the house?

Did you note how many doors or entrances there are to the house?

How many entrances are there?

Were you able to go inside the house?

Please explain what you did inside the house.

In terms of the fire, what did you observe?

Were you able to form opinions regarding the origin and cause of the fire at 117 Jump Street?

Are your opinions within a reasonable degree of scientific certainty?

What is your opinion regarding the origin of the fire?

Please explain what you mean by a "multiple origin fire."

Captain, how is it you concluded fires originated at four different places in the house?

Did you take photos during your investigation?

(showing photos to opposing counsel) May the record reflect I am showing opposing counsel composite exhibit 7, which we have stipulated to.

May I approach the witness? (approaching witness)

Captain Barton, I am showing you composite exhibit 7. Are these the photos you took inside the house at 117 Jump Street on August 3rd and 4th?

(Putting photos up on screen) May the witness step down?

Beginning with the photo labeled 7-A, please tell us wat we are seeing.
> (using the composite exhibit, the witness identifies fires in 4 different rooms)

For purposes of the record, have you identified the northeast bedroom, the northwest bedroom, the kitchen, and the living room?

When you state there is no connection between these fires, did you consider the possibility of fire moving beneath the floor?

Please explain how you ruled that out.

Do you have an opinion, within a reasonable degree of scientific certainty, on the cause of these fires?

What is your opinion?

Please explain how you concluded each of these fires were intentionally set.

What are burn patterns?

What is the significance of the burn patterns in each of these four rooms we discussed a few moments ago?

I want to ask you about accelerants. In terms of fire investigation, what are accelerants?

Do you always find evidence of accelerants?

What are some of the reasons you may not find traces or residue of accelerants during your investigation?

Did you consider the possibility of an electrical fire in the house?

Please explain how you ruled that out.

CHALLENGING EXPERT WITNESS TESTIMONY.

Expert testimony may be challenged as a preliminary matter if the foundation is lacking. One side may challenge the other side's expert based on inadequate credentials or an insufficient level of knowledge, skill, training, or experience. Like any other testimony, expert testimony should assist the jurors in resolving an issue in the case. It should be reliable. It should be presented in a juror-friendly way. The expert's opinions should be within the expert's identified area of expertise. The expert should add something to the case that cannot be had from the available fact witnesses or other evidence.

POTENTIAL AREAS FOR CROSS EXAMINATION OF EXPERTS.

Weak credentials
Contrast between credentials of opposing experts
Bias (party)
Bias (the science or technology)
Incentive (fees)
Incentive (business relationships)
Insufficient knowledge of the facts
Authoritative sources (learned treatises)

The cross examiner should select areas that work in the context of the case. There will rarely be a case where the opponent's expert is vulnerable in several areas. It is better to maintain credibility by choosing a path of cross examination that has the most traction. This is especially important in cases where the other side's expert is helpful to the cross-examiner's side as well. Most experts acknowledge helpful facts and concepts during cross examination because it is necessary to do so as a member of the scientific community.

SAMPLE EXPERT WITNESS CROSS EXAMINATION IN MEDICAL NEGLIGENCE/WRONGFUL DEATH CASE.

Dr. Cowart, you make mistakes, right?

Everyone makes mistakes?

You have made mistakes in your professional practice?

You have been mistaken in your professional opinions, haven't you?

Your opinion must be based on the facts, right?

We don't know how long Mr. Lane was unconscious before the paramedics arrived, do we?

The first time we know is the time of the 911 call, correct?

We know it took another 13 minutes for the paramedics to get to the house?

We know Mr. Lane had ingested 80 milligrams of oxycodone?

That were originally in pill form?

The pill form is oxycontin, correct?

Two oxycontin pills?

40 milligrams each?

These pills had been cooked into liquid form, yes?

And injected?

That is not the proper method of using the drug oxycontin, is it?

It's a prescription drug, correct?

It's not a recreational drug, is it?

It's meant to be taken in pill form?

It's meant to be absorbed into the bloodstream over a period of time, correct?

One dose is meant to be absorbed over a 12-hour period?

When the paramedics arrived, Mr. Lane had less than 3 breaths per minute, correct?

That's what "agonal breathing" means, correct?

We know that narcan was administered in this case, don't we?

That's another name for the drug naloxin?

Narcan is used to reverse the effects of a narcotic overdose, correct?

We don't know that it had any effect on Mr. Lane, do we?

You are assuming that the narcan had an effect?

There is nothing in the notes to indicate it had an effect, is there?

Let's talk about the active ingredient, oxycodone. Oxycodone is a depressant, correct?

A narcotic?

It affects the central nervous system?

It is like morphine in that respect, correct?

It can lead to unconsciousness?

It can cause a person to stop breathing?

It can stop the flow of oxygen to the brain?

Brain function requires oxygen, doesn't it?

At some point, if the brain is deprived of oxygen, brain damage occurs?

The body begins to shut down?

The vital organs begin to fail?

At some point, the damage becomes irreversible?

Death can occur from an overdose of oxycontin, correct?

SAMPLE CROSS OF FINGERPRINT ANALYST.

Mr. Reese, your agency is a law enforcement agency, correct?

Your lab assists local law enforcement departments?

You are not subject to proficiency testing by any outside agency, correct?

Or any private company?

You were aware this was a homicide case?

You knew that before you began your work?

You were given a set of Mr. Lawrence's known prints, correct?

And asked if you could find a match?

Your work in this case is limited to the lab?

You are an analyst?

You are not a crime scene technician?

You are not a crime scene specialist?

You didn't process any surface in this case, did you?

Processing is not within your expertise, is it?

You had no part in lifting any latent prints in this case, did you?

Known prints and latent prints are different, correct?

Known prints are taken or rolled under controlled conditions?

All ten fingers, correct?

And both palms?

Latent lifts are not like known prints, are they?

It's fair to say that latent prints can be challenging?

You must first question whether you have enough of a print to evaluate, right?

Imperfections in latent impressions complicate the analysis?

Smudges complicate the analysis?

Differences in pressure applied as the print was left?

Any sort of distortion complicates the analysis, right?

Mr. Reese, you can't superimpose a latent over a known print and get a perfect match, can you?

Earlier, you referred to latent print examination as a science?

But your conclusions are subjective, aren't they?

Your conclusions tell us nothing about when a print was left, correct?

They tell us nothing about the circumstances, either?

Let's return to the process of comparison. In the United States, there is no standard for the number of points necessary for an identification, correct?

So, it's a judgement call by the examiner?

Given all the training and education that you mentioned earlier, you are aware that mistakes have been made in print identification, correct?

You are familiar with the 2009 National Academy of Science's Report on Forensic Science?

Specifically, you are familiar with the NAS findings regarding the accuracy and reliability of friction ridge analysis?

According to the NAS, a "zero error rate" for this type of comparison is scientifically implausible, correct?

You are a member of the International Association of Identification, correct?

You mentioned earlier that certification by the IAI is considered the gold standard?

The IAI suggests that examiners document their work, correct?

This information is posted on the IAI website, isn't it?

You didn't make any notes about your comparisons in this case, did you?

Nothing about the loops and whorls you referred to earlier, correct?

Nothing about ridge detail analysis?

Sample cross of defense psychologist:

Dr. Bates, you are not a medical doctor, correct?

You don't prescribe medications?

You are not a psychiatrist?

Most of your work has been with juveniles, correct?

Most of your research has centered on early adolescence?

The defendant in this case is 28, right?

Doctor, the facts are important to you in your field, correct?

Very important?

If you have inaccurate facts, it would affect your opinion?

The same with incomplete facts, right?

In this case, you interviewed the defendant's family members, right?

All of your face-to-face interviews were with family members?

Sample cross of arrogant witness:

> Doctor Jones, when you stated earlier, "I am unable to provide an explanation for that," it means you don't know, correct?

> In your direct testimony, you stated "there could be a variety of different reasons for that." That also means you don't know, correct?

Case analysis must include relevance and admissibility.

Character evidence is not admissible unless character is at issue.

Character traits other than truthfulness are usually not at issue.

Evidence must be considered in the context of the entire case.

Good lawyers can spot evidence issues.

Good lawyers edit the opponent's case through motion practice.

Lawyers are obligated to protect clients through objections.

Issues must be properly preserved for appeal.

Verdicts are based on what jurors see and hear in the courtroom and on what they *don't* see or hear. To handle cases effectively, a lawyer must learn to spot evidentiary issues. Issues will appear in the process of investigating a case and developing theories favorable to a client. Throughout the investigation stage, potential admissibility issues should be noted. It is not enough to learn things which support the client's position. *Admissible* proof is necessary for trial.

While preparing a case, a good lawyer *assumes* there will be well-prepared and capable counsel on the other side. Nothing should be taken for granted. Every fact that needs to be in the case should be tested for admissibility. Lawyers are professionally obligated to make and respond to objections. Judges have the discretion to allow or exclude evidence. These are two of many reasons why it is important to conduct a thorough fact investigation before setting a firm trial date.

Once discovery has come full-circle, every part of the case should be "pre-tried" for admissibility. For example, key facts may surface through second or even third-hand witnesses. Hearsay may be a barrier to proving the facts unless a competent witness or another form of proof can be located. Additional time may be needed to identify a proper records custodian and obtain records. Sometimes a witness with first-hand or personal knowledge must be located. For some issues, a qualified expert may be necessary. Lawyers should develop every theory of admissibility for all facts which support the case. They should also be prepared to argue principles of state and constitutional law supporting their positions.

During trial, new issues appear. It is not possible to anticipate every possible objection, response, or evidentiary dilemma. Trial lawyers must understand evidence well enough to think on their feet. Witnesses say unexpected things. In the blink of an eye, an opposing lawyer may ask a question or make an argument that impacts the fairness of the proceedings. There is not time to flip through caselaw or evidence guides. Lawyers must *listen to everything* during trial to make sure objections are made in a timely fashion and error is preserved for appeal.

CHARACTER EVIDENCE IS NOT ADMISSIBLE UNLESS CHARACTER IS AT ISSUE.

Lawyers sometimes struggle with evidence because they don't recognize the difference between action facts and character facts. In terms of admissibility, action or event facts are usually not controversial. A witness who saw someone driving a car into oncoming traffic or firing a handgun is an action witness. Action witnesses can almost always tell the jurors what they observed. Controversy arises when, instead of telling the jury what the defendant *did*, the witness tells the jury *what kind of person* the defendant is. Character evidence is only admissible when a character trait is at issue.

A witness's truthfulness is always at issue. Jurors must weigh the credibility of witnesses in any type of case. It is important for lawyers to challenge the credibility of witnesses who have harmful testimony. State and federal rules specify the *ways* lawyers are permitted to explore this character trait. Although truthfulness is always relevant, lawyers do not have the freedom to attack opposing witnesses with abandon.

Outside the boundary of truthfulness, character evidence is presumptively inadmissible. Jurors are not allowed to decide legal claims based on the likeability of the litigants. This concept is very important for trial lawyers. Appellate courts across the country review verdicts on a regular basis because inadmissible character evidence was allowed in front of a jury. Many of these cases are reversed.

Character traits beyond truthfulness must be relevant in the *specific* context of a lawsuit to support the admission of this controversial type of evidence. For example, evidence demonstrating a person's violent or peaceful character is relevant on the issue of self-defense. Evidence of a defendant's prior bad acts or prior similar crimes may be admissible as proof of identity, intent, motive, knowledge, or plan. A witness's prior sexual conduct is usually irrelevant and inadmissible. However, evidence of a prior consensual sexual relationship between an accuser and a defendant may be relevant on the issue of consent.

In these circumstances, judges must weigh the probative value of the character evidence against its inflammatory nature or the danger of unfair prejudice. Jurors should hear *relevant* evidence *if* it is not so inflammatory that it becomes a distraction or provokes a verdict based on anger. The party offering controversial character evidence should be prepared to argue 1) the specific purpose for the evidence and 2) its importance in the case.

This area of evidence must be mastered by lawyers who go to court. It is especially important for prosecutors and defense attorneys. Trials are about conduct, not popularity. The constitution does not permit the loss of liberty or property based on personality. Name-calling is almost always objectionable. Other forms of character evidence must be considered on a case-by-case basis.

Good lawyers train themselves to spot issues and prepare to address them before trial. They pre-try their own evidence to make sure they can get important facts admitted. They also pre-try the opponent's evidence to make sure they are ready to object.

Everything heard or seen by jurors should 1) tend to prove or disprove a charge, claim, or defense, or 2) relate to credibility. Relevance is a low threshold, but it is an important one. Lawyers should view the evidence within this framework of charges, claims and defenses. What issues are raised in the pleadings? What jury instructions apply in the case? Relevance depends on context, and context depends on the facts and legal issues in the case.

In a different world, jurors might learn everything imaginable about a case and the people involved in it. In an American courtroom, jurors are expected to learn everything that is relevant in a proscribed legal context, based on concepts of fairness and reliability.

Before trial, lawyers spend much of their time gathering facts. They gather all kinds of facts– historical facts, background facts, eye-witness facts, bias facts, scientific facts, contradictory facts, and ultimate facts. When they have gathered all the facts, they must thoughtfully select those which prove the client's case or disprove the opponent's. They must consider credibility facts in addition to facts which strictly prove or disprove claims. Good lawyers try to "edit" the other party's evidence with proper objections and motions.

At trial, a good lawyer is ready to relate specific evidence to claims, charges, defenses, or credibility in the context of the case. If a relevance objection is made, the lawyer offering the evidence should be prepared to respond. For example:

It's relevant to:

negligence
state of mind
notice
intent
consent
credibility
motive/incentive
bias
(monetary) value
Impairment
identity
It shows lack of mistake

It shows guilty knowledge

It shows a plan

It's relevant as fair response to facts offered by the opponent (the opened door)

Sometimes presumptively inadmissible evidence is made relevant and admissible because the opposing party has "opened the door." If one side ventures into areas the opposing side has previously been prevented from addressing, fairness may require the judge to allow a response.

MOTIONS.

While preparing, lawyers spot issues that need to be resolved before the trial begins. Good lawyers want to know in advance whether their evidence and witnesses will be allowed. It is best to have as much certainty as possible before investing in process service, witness fees, exhibits, calendar time, preparation, and hours of work. Motion hearings are a means of getting as much certainty as possible in advance of trial.

Some motion hearings are like mini trials. Written motions are filed, and hearing time is scheduled with the judge. Witnesses are subpoenaed for the hearing, and testimony is presented prior to argument. Local rules and administrative orders often dictate the timing of motion hearings.

Motion practice separates the highly skilled lawyer from the amateur. In complex cases, lawyers often spend hours deciding what needs to be raised pretrial, drafting motions, deciding what evidence needs to be presented, and doing research to support the motions.

If the facts underlying the issue are not in dispute, the judge *may* be able to rule without hearing testimony. Motions that don't call for live testimony are often argued immediately prior to trial. For example, anticipatory objections for relevance or hearsay are often handled in a motion *in limine*. This is a way of getting a pretrial order excluding irrelevant or unfairly prejudicial facts or hearsay.

Intelligent, strategic motion practice is essential for trial lawyers. Is there an issue? Will it be necessary to present evidence before the judge can rule? What is the most appropriate and persuasive way to present the issue to the judge?

It is the responsibility of the moving party to determine whether live testimony or other evidence is necessary for the court to resolve an issue. Opponents are entitled to reasonable notice, so they can prepare to address the motion. Will testimony be necessary? Can the judge rule on the issue based on depositions, affidavits, or the pleadings alone? All parties should be aware of the standard of proof applicable to the issue, and which party bears the burden of proof.

In criminal cases, the defendant has a constitutional right to be present for all critical stages of the proceedings. This is another reason why planning is important for motion practice.

For some issues, once preliminary facts are established, the burden of proof may shift to the opposing party. For example, warrantless searches are presumptively unlawful, so once the defense presents evidence that a warrantless seizure occurred, the government must come forward with evidence of an exception to the warrant requirement. It is important to be thoroughly familiar with the law pertaining to the issue before launching into a pretrial motion.

Depending on the complexity of an issue, some motion hearings last for several days. Other motions can be addressed in a matter of minutes.

EXAMPLES OF DIFFERENT TYPES OF MOTIONS.

Personal injury case:

> The defendant makes a timely discovery request for medical records of the plaintiff. The plaintiff fails to provide the records. Defense counsel files a motion to compel production. The lawyers have a brief hearing with the judge. The judge rules on the motion after reviewing the pleadings and the motion. In some states, if the judge finds the losing party had no good faith basis to oppose the motion, the prevailing party may be entitled to costs and fees associated with the motion.

Murder case:

> The defense claims that incriminating statements were taken in violation of the defendant's constitutional rights under the 5th and 6th Amendments to the United States Constitution. The defense files a motion to suppress the statements and schedules a hearing. The judge hears testimony from police officers and the defendant at the hearing. Lawyers for each side present argument.

The judge then reviews case law submitted by both parties and takes the issue under advisement for a few days prior to issuing a ruling.

Medical malpractice case:

The case is being tried. The defendant moves for a directed verdict after the plaintiff announces rest. The motion is based upon evidence presented thus far in the trial and a standard set forth in the rules. The issue is whether sufficient evidence of causation exists to submit the case to a jury. Both sides offer case law. The judge hears argument at side-bar, in chambers, or excuses the jurors for argument in open court. The judge then rules based on the plaintiff's evidence and the standard as set out in the rules of civil procedure.

Aggravated battery case:

The prosecution anticipates that defense witnesses may testify to highly prejudicial evidence about the victim's character. Shortly before opening statements, the prosecution makes an oral motion to exclude the evidence, and the defense responds. The judge considers the specific nature of the evidence, listens to the arguments of both parties, and makes a ruling on the spot.

Alternatively, the judge defers ruling on admissibility of the challenged evidence until she has heard testimony from witnesses and feels more comfortable determining its relevance. She may do this with a proffer, so she can hear the testimony outside the presence of the jurors and make a ruling.

Products liability case:

The plaintiffs sue a drug manufacturer after suffering serious complications from medication. The defendant claims that the plaintiff's expert testimony regarding causation should be excluded for failure of the expert to follow basic methodology required in toxic tort cases. The defendant files a written motion to exclude the testimony pursuant to principles set forth in *Daubert v. Merrell Dow Pharmaceuticals, Inc.*, 509 U.S. 579 (1993). Both sides present numerous witnesses and oral and written arguments. The judge takes the matter under advisement and issues a ruling at the next case management conference.

Armed robbery case:

At trial status conference, the defense makes an oral motion to exclude hearsay testimony from a key prosecution witness. The motion is based on the hearsay rule. The prosecution concedes the hearsay issue but argues an investigator is attempting to locate a non-hearsay witness for the same evidence. The judge grants the motion and gives the prosecution twenty-four hours to produce the non-hearsay witness and make the witness available to the defense.

Personal injury case:

The defendant asks for a special verdict form based on the number of defendants in the case (some have settled). The judge hears argument from both parties, reviews the pleadings and other documents filed by the parties, and the case law. The judge then rules.

Cyber stalking case:

The defendant requests a special jury instruction. The judge hears argument from both parties and reviews case law. The judge grants the motion conditionally. The ruling will ultimately depend on the type of evidence presented at the trial.

OBJECTIONS.

Lawyers *must* make objections on behalf of their clients. There are two very important reasons for objecting.

First, jurors should not hear irrelevant or unfairly prejudicial information during the trial. Once they hear it, they may be unable or unwilling to disregard it. Verdicts based on irrelevant or inflammatory evidence are unfair.

Secondly, excepting fundamental error, appellate courts will only consider issues *raised* during trial and *preserved* for appeal. Lawyers are expected to raise issues with the trial judge when the case is still before the jury. If an issue is properly raised during the trial, the judge has an opportunity to exclude unfair evidence or admit important, relevant evidence before the jurors deliberate.

Appellate courts review adverse *rulings* on issues. Appellate judges aren't expected to speculate on whether a party forgot to raise an issue or on what the trial judge might have done if presented with the issue.

Well-prepared lawyers can anticipate most objections. They prepare to make objections, and they prepare to defend admissibility of evidence they will offer. Relevance is the threshold issue. Does the information *tend* to prove or disprove a material fact in the case? A tendency is enough. Litigants are not limited to the bare story facts. Does the information relate to the credibility or bias of witnesses? How is it probative? If it is difficult to answer these questions, the evidence is likely inadmissible.

Some relevant evidence is subject to exclusion because its probative value is low and the danger of unfair prejudice is high.

During witness examinations, lawyers have an obligation to listen to the opposing side. Questions may be objectionable based on form or because they call for objectionable answers. Sometimes an appropriate question is answered with objectionable information. Either way, a timely objection should be made. The objection should be as specific as possible. All proper grounds for objection should be included when addressing the court. "Piecemeal" objections are not timely.

Some lawyers fall into the bad habit of making "speaking" objections rather than training themselves to identify the grounds for objection succinctly. A speaking objection is one with argument or discussion as to why certain evidence should be excluded. If it is necessary to present argument on an objection, a lawyer should ask to be heard *before* trial or, if it is too late for that option, at side bar. From counsel table, objections should be short and concise.

Speaking objections can add hours of time in trial and turn the process into an ordeal for everyone. Sometimes bench conferences are necessary. At other times, when the basis for the objection is clear, a one-or-two-word objection should be made from the table. It is objectionable to argue about *admissibility* in front of jurors. Generally, judges don't permit speaking objections in open court.

Objections should be made whenever these two criteria are met: 1) there is a basis for the objection under state or federal law, and 2) the objection is in the interests of the client.

Objections should be made with a professional tone. They should not be tentative. They should not be rude.

It is important to obtain a ruling before moving on in the trial. Adverse rulings should be handled with grace. If a ruling excludes favorable evidence, the side who wanted the evidence should make sure there is some record of what would have been presented. This is called a proffer. If the evidence is not already part of the record, lawyers should ask to read or state the information to the court reporter or to submit the content in a pre-existing form (deposition excerpt, business record, witness statement).

Lawyers have a professional obligation to make proper objections on behalf of a client. A lawyer should never fail to protect a client because of concerns that objecting interrupts the other lawyer or that jurors may think it is rude to object. In most jurisdictions, there is a standard preliminary instruction for jurors to the effect that lawyers are trained in evidence and may need to make objections during the trial. [12]

Contemporaneous, specific objections are required to preserve most issues for appeal. [13] Appellate courts have acknowledged that diligent efforts to preserve error may offend or alienate jurors, but objections are still necessary for the protection of a client's appellate rights. [14]

An objecting (or responding) lawyer should make sure the judge has the necessary facts and context to make a ruling. Trial judges are often unfamiliar with cases prior to trial. There are times when a bench conference is necessary. Judges must sometimes hear argument to determine whether evidence should be admitted.

If highly emotional or controversial evidence is important in a case, the side offering the evidence should be prepared to explain its relevance and probative value. If there is an objection, the side offering the evidence needs to persuade the judge that the evidence has a lawful purpose and will not be offered for (unlawful) inflammatory value.

In addition to objecting, a lawyer should move for mistrial when the fairness of the trial has been called into question. Broadly speaking, evidence or arguments that threaten a constitutional right justify a motion for mistrial.

SPECIFIC OBJECTIONS: RELEVANCE (FRE 401-404).

When a question calls for information which is *not probative* of any *issue* in the case, or an answer contains similar content, an objection is proper. Witness

---

12 *See* Florida Standard Jury Instruction 2.1: "The attorneys are trained in the rules of evidence and trial procedure, and it is their duty to make all objections they feel are proper..." This instruction should be requested by counsel if not otherwise given.

13 FRE 103; parallel state provisions.

14 *See* Bocher and McMurray v. Glass and Glass, 874 So.2d 701(Fla. App. 1st Dist. 2004).

credibility is always relevant, but evidence rules limit the ways credibility can be attacked or supported.

Relevance issues often arise when witnesses start volunteering how they *feel* or what they *think* as opposed to what they *saw* or what they *know*. Jurors usually need to deal with objective facts. Subjective feelings or viewpoints of witnesses are usually irrelevant. One exception is information relevant to bias. This is usually elicited during cross examination of an opponent's witnesses. There are other exceptions, like a robbery victim's fear (an element of robbery) or pain and suffering evidence (damages).

Character evidence may also be relevant to incentive or motive. For example, a prosecution witness's pending charges are relevant to the witness's incentive to testify favorably for the government. Under other circumstances, the same evidence would be inadmissible.

Lawyers should be wary when a witness begins to give character evidence. The character trait for truthfulness of testifying witnesses is always relevant. Other character traits must be at issue in a law suit before character evidence is relevant. Although it may seem important as background, character evidence is *legally* relevant in very limited circumstances.[15]

For example, the victim of a credit card scam may have a reputation for violence, but his violent nature is irrelevant to whether his credit card information was stolen. If the same person is the complaining witness in a shooting case, and the defendant was aware of the violent reputation of the witness or specific acts of violence by the witness at the time of the shooting, the evidence may be highly relevant to self-defense.

Many cases are reversed because jurors were permitted to consider irrelevant character evidence. Others are reversed because a party was prevented from offering relevant character evidence.

Relevance issues also arise when witnesses make overbroad statements or offer personal opinions.[16]

Jurors are asked to decide issues based on proven facts and applicable law. They are not supposed to decide cases based on anger, sympathy, speculation, like, or dislike. Any time a party offers evidence *solely* to inflame the passions of the jurors or evoke sympathy, it is objectionable.

---

15   Dawson v. Delaware, 503 U.S. 159 (1992); Thompson v. Bowie, 71 U.S. 463 (1866).

16   Griffin v. Florida, 872 So.2d 998 (Fla. App. 4th Dist. 2004).

HEARSAY (FRE 801-807).

As a rule, witnesses are not permitted to repeat statements they heard or made at some point prior to the trial. American legal philosophy recognizes the value of *contemporaneous* cross examination, so out-of-court statements are subject to the hearsay rule. If the statement is an assertion of fact (capable of being true or false), and it is offered at trial *for its truth*, it is hearsay and objectionable on statutory and constitutional grounds.[17] Testimony should be based on personal knowledge rather than the repetition of things someone said earlier, including things the testifying witness said earlier.

Many out-of-court statements are admissible for some purpose other than to prove their *truth*. These statements do not meet the definition of hearsay, so they are not objectionable on hearsay grounds. For example, prior statements that are inconsistent with a witness's courtroom testimony are admissible for purposes of attacking the credibility of the witness. Some out-of-court statements are admissible because they prove notice or knowledge of a fact or circumstance. Other statements are admissible to explain why a person acted in a certain way, commonly referred to as "effect on listener." Out-of-court statements are only admissible for their effect on the listener if the listener's conduct or motivation is at issue in the case.

Some hearsay is admissible as an exception or exclusion to the rule. Party admissions are an example. Because it is generally not allowed, lawyers offering hearsay should be prepared to defend its admissibility (as an exception or exclusion) under state or federal law.

LEADING DURING DIRECT EXAMINATION (FRE 611(c)).

Lawyers should not coach their own witnesses during direct examination. The opposing lawyer should listen to make sure the witness is not being fed answers. Some lawyers make too many leading objections, and some make too few.

Generally, if the direct examiner has a *pattern* of leading his witness or asks leading questions on the disputed issues, a leading objection should be made.

---

17   Crawford v. Washington, 541 U. S. 36, 124 S. Ct. 1354, 158 L. Ed. 2nd 177 (2004).

ARGUMENTATIVE CROSS-EXAMINATION.

Argumentative cross-examination questions are objectionable. Witnesses are not required to debate the cross examiner. Cross examination is not an opportunity for the opposing lawyer to lecture or scold the witness.

It can also be dangerous for a cross examiner to argue with the other side's witnesses. Whether objected to or not, lawyers who argue with witnesses often lose. By engaging in argument with witnesses during cross examination, a lawyer sends an unintended and unhelpful message to the jury that she *needs* the witness's agreement.

The proper time to argue is during closing.

Rhetorical questions are objectionable. They are not sincerely intended to obtain an admission or denial of fact. Instead, they are usually attempts to bully or spar with a witness. The witness often wins this sort of question.

COMPOUND CROSS-EXAMINATION.

It is unfair and objectionable to expect a "yes" or "no" answer to a *multiple*-part question. The witness may only agree with part of the question. The question is compound if it contains more than one point the witness must concede or deny.

QUESTION ASSUMES FACTS NOT IN EVIDENCE.

It is objectionable to ask questions which assume facts that are not in evidence. Lawyers are not witnesses, and the evidence must come from witnesses or other forms of admitted evidence.

This objection does not pertain to proper, leading cross examination questions. Lawyers often present "new" information in cross examination for purposes of obtaining an admission or concession from the witness. If the questions have a good-faith basis, this is entirely proper.

This objection is not a bar to the use of hypothetical questions with experts. There are circumstances where hypothetical questions are proper and useful in the context of presenting and supporting an expert's opinion. Hypothetical questions are often used in cases where the underlying facts are in dispute.

IMPROPER IMPEACHMENT (FRE 607-610).

Because of its potential impact on witness credibility, impeachment should be fair. Improper impeachment occurs when a lawyer attempts to impeach a witness's truthfulness with prior statements of the witness that are *not* inconsistent with the witness's courtroom testimony. Also, it is improper to impeach a witness's *credibility* with character evidence unrelated to truthfulness, bias, or motive.

It is improper to impeach a witness with collateral facts or issues. The impeachment material must have some connection to the case.

Pending charges, probationary status, or plea agreements of *prosecution* witnesses are relevant for bias, incentive, or motive. This type of credibility evidence is separate from evidence of prior convictions under FRE 609 or parallel state provisions. [18]

CALLS FOR SPECULATION/ SPECULATIVE.

If a witness is guessing or speculating about a fact, she does not have the personal knowledge necessary to testify. Sloppy lawyers sometimes invite this objection by asking a witness for a "best guess" or an "estimate."

NARRATIVE.

Witnesses are expected to answer a series of questions framed by the issues in the case and the rules of evidence. It is objectionable for a witness to "take the floor" by expanding answers into a longer or broader discussion. If a witness continues to talk after the pending question has been fairly answered, there is a risk that the witness will move into irrelevant and harmful information. The lawyer presenting the witness is expected to control the examination by asking questions that call for relevant information and keeping the witness on track.

---

18 Fulton v. Florida, 335 So. 2d 280 (Fla. 1976); Douglas v. Florida, 627 So. 2d 1190 (Fla. App. 1st Dist. 1993); Watson v. Indiana, 507 N.E. 2d 571 (Sup. Ct. Ind. 1987)

CROSS BEYOND/OUTSIDE THE SCOPE OF DIRECT (FRE 611(B)).

Cross-examination is the opportunity to confront and challenge the opponent's witnesses, so the scope is generally broad. The cross examiner should be permitted to explore any matters put into play in direct examination.

Bias, motive, and other credibility evidence is always relevant and therefore always within the scope. A witness's credibility is at issue from the moment testimony begins. The right to a full and fair cross examination has constitutional underpinnings. For these reasons, scope objections are not often granted.

There are limits. A scope objection is proper when the cross examiner moves into areas which are either irrelevant or more appropriately raised in the (cross-examiner's) case-in-chief.

BEST EVIDENCE RULE.

Lawyers should not ask witnesses to discuss, interpret or explain the *contents* of documents, records, or recordings in place of admitting the evidence. An objection is proper when a witness is asked to discuss the contents of documents or other evidence which has not been admitted.

LACK OF FOUNDATION OR INSUFFICIENT FOUNDATION (FRE 901).

Objections for lack of foundation should be made with specificity.[19]

For example, if a witness cannot state that a picture accurately represents the scene at the time of the accident, there is a valid objection to be made. The objection should be, "Objection: There's no showing the exhibit reflects the scene on the accident date." Merely stating, "Objection, no foundation" is insufficient in most jurisdictions.

If the witness instead gives a qualified answer, such as "It looks the same, except it is daylight and the accident was at night," the judge may admit the picture anyway, finding that the difference goes more to weight than admissibility. Admissibility is a lower threshold. Jurors may give the picture less evidentiary

---

19   Jackson v. Florida, 738 So. 2d 382 (Fla. App. 4th Dist. 1999)

value or "weight" because it was taken in the daylight, but the picture is still helpful to understanding the case and deciding the issues. Situations like these are handled on a case-by-case basis.

Through pretrial discovery, lawyers usually know what exhibits or other evidence will be offered by the opposing side. In some circumstances, it is appropriate to stipulate to the admissibility of certain items instead of forcing the opponent to present foundation testimony. If the parties stipulate to certain evidence, the judge should be made aware of the stipulation prior to trial.

If the subject calls for expertise and the witness has not been qualified as an expert, it is proper to object on the basis that the expert foundation is lacking.

ASKED AND ANSWERED.

Once a question has been answered, the lawyer who asked it is expected to move on to another question. During direct examination, it is improper for a lawyer to repeatedly cover the same favorable evidence with the witness.

Lawyers should also move on during cross examination unless the witness is being evasive or simply hasn't answered the question. The cross examiner is entitled to an answer for each proper question. Since witnesses are often evasive during cross examination, judges usually give cross examiners wide latitude. [20]

The cross examiner is also entitled to go into the territory covered in direct examination. A lawyer should not be permitted to use the asked-and-answered objection to prevent full and fair cross examination. For example, a cross examiner may set up an impeachment by locking the witness into something said during direct. This is entirely proper. A cross examiner may explore bias and motive evidence even where the direct examiner attempted to "draw the sting out" by asking about it during direct examination. The cross examiner obviously has different reasons for covering the evidence. Because of the constitutional right to confront and cross examine adverse witnesses, latitude is usually permitted.

---

20 Cross-examiners often zero in on direct exam testimony, *but for a different purpose*, such as setting up an impeachment.

Lawyers must protect the rights of their clients to a fair trial before a *fair and impartial* judge. The constitutional right to a fair trial is only meaningful if the parties are treated fairly by the judge. Judges are sworn to preside and rule with impartial, disinterested attention to the facts and law. As human beings, they sometimes say or do things during a trial that demonstrate favoritism or hostility toward one side. When a judge threatens the fairness of trial proceedings, an objection must be made on behalf of the party whose rights are in jeopardy.

Judges have great power. In ideal circumstances, they command well-deserved respect. It may be awkward or intimidating for a lawyer to object to comments or actions of a judge. Whether pleasant or not, it is necessary to protect a client when the judge steps out of the neutral zone. Judges should appear neutral as to the parties and the outcome of any lawsuit. They should not comment on the credibility of witnesses or say anything which indicates a personal preference for one side or the other. Consider these examples:

> The judge refers to the wife in a dissolution of marriage proceeding as "a queen in a hive."

> The judge constantly interrupts defense counsel's opening statement without any objection from the other side.

OBJECTIONABLE ARGUMENT.

Closing arguments should be based on facts in evidence, reasonable inferences drawn from those facts, and the applicable law. The boundaries for closing are premised on the constitutional right to a fair trial. If jurors consider factors other than the facts and the law of the case, it is unfair. Lawyers who venture outside these boundaries risk error that may result in a reversal. A lawyer may also be subject to disciplinary action for egregious violations during closing argument. Here are several examples of objectionable argument:

LAWYER'S OPINION.

Lawyers may have personal opinions on fault, damages, guilt, or innocence in the cases they try. However, these are not relevant at trial. It is objectionable for a lawyer to inject his personal opinion into closing argument. It is best to play it safe with idiom and take the phrases, "I believe," "I feel," and "I think" out of the trial vocabulary.

VOUCHING FOR WITNESSES OR THE CASE.

(Similar to above) It is improper for a lawyer to vouch for her witnesses or explain that she only takes cases with merit. A lawyer's opinion about the witnesses or the case is irrelevant. It is the *jurors'* opinions that matter. The right to trial by jury is only meaningful if the jurors, and not the party advocates, decide the case. Jurors are entitled to evaluate the credibility of witnesses, the strength of evidence, and the merits of claims, charges, or defenses with their *own* judgment, common sense, and reason.

PERSONAL ATTACKS ON OPPOSING COUNSEL.

Cases should be decided based on the facts and law. One lawyer's opinion of another is irrelevant. Any *genuine* concerns about the conduct of the opposing lawyer should be addressed with the judge at sidebar or with a bar disciplinary committee. A lawyer's negative feeling toward the opposing lawyer is not a matter for the jury.

It is difficult for jurors to do their job when the lawyers create a "combat" atmosphere. It is also unfair when a lawyer tries to turn the trial into a popularity contest.

Jurors are influenced by the behavior of the lawyers in a trial. Lawyers communicate many things about the strengths or weaknesses of the case and their confidence level by the ways they choose to speak and act during the trial. This is a natural part of what trial lawyers do and a natural part of communication. However, deliberate manipulation of the jury by attacking the opposing lawyer is improper.

PERSONAL ATTACKS ON THE OPPOSING PARTY OR WITNESSES.

(Similar to above) Name-calling and irrelevant character attacks on the opposing party or witnesses are objectionable. The only character evidence that can be properly used against a party or a witness is the evidence allowed during testimony.

Lawyers who attempt to gain an unfair advantage by creating a mob mentality in the courtroom or stirring up hatred for the opposing side should be stopped immediately.

MISSTATING THE LAW OR SUGGESTING SOME OF THE LAW SHOULD BE IGNORED.

For obvious reasons, it is improper for a lawyer to mislead jurors on any aspect of the law.

SHIFTING THE BURDEN OF PROOF.

(Similar to above) This issue comes up most often in criminal trials. Prosecutors must remember that defendants are not required to prove innocence. Jurors can reject the testimony of defendants or defense witnesses and still find that the state's evidence fails the reasonable doubt standard. In strictest terms, it is not the prosecution versus the defendant-- it is the prosecution versus a reasonable doubt.

The burden of proof is part of the law in any case, so arguments that mislead jurors about the burden are also misstatements of the law.

COMMENTS ON THE RIGHT TO REMAIN SILENT.

(Related to above) This is an issue in criminal trials. The defendant does not have to testify, present evidence, or "answer" the prosecution's evidence. The prosecutor should not call attention to the proper exercise of this constitutional right.

FLAG WAVING, APPEALS TO PATRIOTISM OR THE "CONSCIENCE OF THE COMMUNITY".

It is improper to appeal to the jurors' sense of patriotism or suggest it is their patriotic duty to find in favor of one side over the other.

ARGUMENTS THAT SEND A MESSAGE.

Aside from cases where punitive damages are at issue, verdicts are not "messages" and lawyers are not entitled to ask jurors to "send a message" by their verdict. Prevailing public opinion is irrelevant in a trial. The community has not been sworn to hear the case. The jurors have that job. This type of argument is highly improper. It brings vigilantism into the trial process.

GOLDEN RULE ARGUMENT.

(Related to above) Lawyers should never ask jurors to put themselves in the shoes of the plaintiff, the victim, or the defendant. "Golden rule" arguments improperly shift jurors away from the evidence in the trial and into a subjective process of deciding what *they* would have done or how *they* would have felt if they were one of the litigants. The trial isn't about what might happen to someone else. It's about what has been proven (by evidence) to have already happened.

Broadly, the golden rule objection applies to any arguments intended to inflame the jurors or draw them away from the evidence and the law. Golden rule violations make it more likely the case will be decided based on anger, sympathy, or a non-existent "what-if-that-were-me" scenario.

The proper way to engage the jurors' experience is to fall back on a standard jury instruction. For example, in many jurisdictions, jurors are instructed that they can rely on their own experience and common sense when *weighing and evaluating the evidence* in the case.

ARGUING FACTS OUTSIDE THE EVIDENCE.

This objection is proper when a lawyer adds facts during closing that were not part of the trial evidence. If a lawyer simply mis-states what a witness said, the judge will usually instruct jurors to rely on their own memories about the testimony. In contrast, the objection is important when a lawyer brings entirely new information to the jurors during closing.

PUTTING THE CASE TOGETHER

Organize trial materials in a logical way.

Build the case before bringing it to court.

Knowing the case is different from memorizing the case.

Work backwards from jury instructions to jury selection.

Start and end with strong witnesses.

Realize the value of neutral witnesses and physical evidence.

Plan for mid-trial motions and the charge conference.

Think of the whole picture, not just the details.

ORGANIZE LOGICALLY.

There are many ways to organize trial materials. The goal is to make them *readily accessible* during trial. Some lawyers bring their computers into the courtroom. Materials needed for trial should also be printed and organized in labeled folders or a loose-leaf notebook.

The courtroom is a special kind of theater. It is not a law office. The jury is a constant and important audience. Lawyers should not have their faces hidden behind computers during trial. If it is necessary to use a computer during trial, co-counsel should assist.

What is the best order of witnesses? What are the thresholds for mid-trial motions? Are the themes natural? Will the direct and cross examinations support the themes? Is all the necessary evidence available? Are the witnesses ready?

It is best to lead off with an event witness. An event witness is a witness who is either involved in the action of the case or very close to it, an eye witness.

PREPARATION DOES NOT MEAN MEMORIZATION.

Canned presentations are not interesting or persuasive. The biggest risk of over-scripting is the failure to grasp what is happening moment to moment in the trial.

Inexperienced lawyers are often tempted to draft word-for-word scripts for the courtroom. Scripts shackle a lawyer to the *pretrial case.* Bullet-point notes give lawyers more room to be genuine and engaging. Lawyers who speak directly and spontaneously to jurors demonstrate true knowledge of the case. They are free from scripts. This gives them authority in the courtroom. They make eye contact with jurors and witnesses. They *listen.* They are in the moment. They are aware of the case the same way jurors are aware of it.

To prepare effectively, an outline format is helpful. Outlines force lawyers to speak with spontaneity while ensuring that nothing will be left out. Outlines are easy to revise on short notice. During trial, lawyers must be flexible. Revisions must be made quickly based on changes in the testimony or rulings on evidence. Outlines should be as simple as possible.

Some lawyers begin trial preparation by outlining their opening statements. Others begin with closing arguments. Closing arguments must be based on the evidence presented, so it makes good sense to start with closing and work backwards. Lawyers who follow this path can make sure each point that needs to be argued will be covered in their direct and cross examinations.

WORK BACKWARDS FROM JURY *INSTRUCTIONS* TO JURY *SELECTION*.

Broadly, the case should be built from jury instructions backwards to jury selection. The laws of the case demand attention. At least one party in the case must present proof on each element and satisfy a burden. When all the witnesses and all the facts have been considered, ideas about jury selection will begin to take shape.

Impeachment materials and case law should be organized by witness and issue. For example, deposition pages, lines, and numbers should be easy to find for impeachment. Pace is important, so any necessary documents or exhibits should be readily available during the witness examination.

START AND END WITH STRONG WITNESSES.

The order of proof is important. What is the most juror-friendly order? A story witness is a good witness to call first. Key players and eye witnesses can do a lot to persuade jurors and get them engaged in the case. What witness order will make the most sense, given the role and knowledge of each witness? How can the case-in-chief be structured so that the first and last witnesses will be powerful and memorable?

NEUTRAL WITNESSES AND PHYSICAL EVIDENCE ARE HIGH-VALUE RESOURCES.

Neutral witnesses and physical evidence can strengthen a case and give it added dimension. Neutral witnesses can restore the jurors' confidence in a case suffering from credibility-compromised litigants. With any non-essential witness, a cost-benefit analysis should be done. A neutral witness who is helpful without adding potential complications should be included in the line-up.

If there is physical evidence, it is helpful to get it in front of the jury early.

During a trial, lawyers may ask the court to dismiss charges or claims or to enter judgment in favor of their side as to certain claims before the case is given to the jury.[21] In criminal trials, the defense may move for a judgment of acquittal when the prosecution's evidence is *legally* insufficient. Reasonable doubt is always a matter for jurors, so judges cannot direct a verdict for the prosecution. Here are some things to keep in mind when planning for mid-trial motions:

Civil plaintiffs and prosecutors must make sure their cases can *survive* a motion. Evidence supporting the elements of each claim or charge must be presented during the case-in-chief. Good lawyers check to make sure they have covered each element before excusing witnesses and announcing "rest."

When moving for a judgment of acquittal (criminal defense) or directed verdict (civil), the *credibility* of the evidence is not the issue. The issue is legal sufficiency as opposed to credibility. Excepting extreme cases, jurors weigh credibility (not the judge).

PREPARE FOR THE CHARGE CONFERENCE. THE JURY
INSTRUCTIONS AND THE VERDICT FORM SHOULD BE CLEAR,
ACCURATE, AND NEUTRAL.

It is important to anticipate the *exact* law the jurors will hear at the close of the trial. Jury instructions are the law in trial form. Most instructions come directly from statutes and codes. They define crimes or torts, standards of care, damages, defenses, and burdens of proof.

The instructions will be used by jurors as they weigh and compare the evidence and ultimately decide who should prevail. The law of the case also dictates the scope and type of facts that are relevant in the trial.

Depending on the type of case and the jurisdiction, some judges give the jurors instructions early in the process. Sometimes lawyers ask the judge to instruct the jurors as early as jury selection. In all cases, the instructions are important. They should not be taken for granted.

Lawyers generally assist the trial judge with the task of determining the proper jury instructions for each case. There are standard jury instructions for

---

21   FRCP 50; FRCRP 29; Fla.R.Crim.P. 3.380; Fla.R.Civ.P. 1.480.

most types of cases[22], but lawyers sometimes need to request special instructions based on specific evidence or issues.

Jurors should be provided with accurate, complete, and neutral explanations of the laws that apply in the case. Jury instructions are notorious for being confusing and difficult to understand. The facts of the case must be viewed in a legal context, so lawyers should prepare to incorporate key legal concepts in their openings (minimally if at all) and closings (more). They should also be prepared to request special instructions where needed.

It is important to object to incomplete, inaccurate, or misleading instructions.

At some point prior to closing arguments, most judges hold a "charge conference." This is an opportunity for the judge and lawyers to review proposed instructions for the case. The charge conference should be of record. It is often held in chambers. In the event a requested instruction is denied or challenged instructions are allowed, an appellate record should be made. Lawyers should also make objections on the record at the time challenged instructions are provided to the jurors.

Judges instruct jurors by reading the law in open court. They may also provide the instructions in writing.[23] In some jurisdictions, jury instructions must be provided in written form in addition to being read by the judge.[24]

The verdict form should be carefully considered. It should clearly and accurately set out each question the jurors are required to answer. Judges often ask the lawyers in a case to submit a proposed verdict form. If a party has objections to the verdict form, these must be made in a timely manner for purposes of appeal.

THINK OF THE WHOLE PICTURE, NOT JUST THE DETAILS.

Good lawyers keep the big picture in mind. Testimony and rulings are never completely predictable. There are many variables. Some witnesses will be more

---

22 The Florida Supreme Court and other state courts adopt and approve standardized instructions, both general and specific to case type. Instructions are often challenged on appeal and are periodically modified based upon changes to the law and appellate challenges.

23 Fla.R.Crim.P. 3.390; Fla.R.Civ.P. 1.470(b); FRCP 51.

24 For instance, in capital cases. Fla.R.Crim.P. 3.390(b).

helpful than expected and others will not deliver the strong facts they seemed to know before trial.

Sometimes jurors fall by the wayside and alternate jurors end up in deliberations. Each juror will see things through a different prism, based on different backgrounds and experiences. Every favorable point and every likeable witness is important.

Lawyers should go into trial prepared to promise, prove, and persuade. Nothing should be taken for granted. Each part of the trial should be considered in concert with the other parts. Strong cases hang together much better than cases resting on a single witness or one great cross examination point.

It is a lawyer's job to get the case to the jurors in the best shape possible. Small details or points held dear by the lawyers may not be important in the jury room. Whatever the ups and downs, a good trial lawyer maintains a positive, straightforward approach to the case from start to finish.

Closing Argument

Now that the case has played out in the courtroom, where is the jury?

How should the case be decided, and *why* should it be decided that way?

What are the best arguments, and what facts can be drawn in to support each one?

What are the powerful aspects of the case?

Who has more facts?

Who has stronger facts?

Who has more credibility?

Who has the burden?

Persuasive arguments are justice-driven.

Stay inside the evidence and the law.

Try the *case* (not the opposing attorney).

AT CLOSING, WHERE IS THE JURY?

To bring jurors to the client's side for deliberations, a lawyer must first have a sense of where they *are.* They are no longer on the way to the courthouse for jury selection, wondering what the case will be about. They have already experienced the case, with all the emotion, tedium, boredom, drama, humor, novelty, data, trivia, color, sadness, or excitement to be found in it.

The testimony is part of the immediate past. The jurors have already developed feelings and opinions about the credibility of the witnesses, the strengths and weaknesses on each side, and the issues. It is reasonable to expect jurors already have ideas about the verdict. It is likely they know how they want to vote, and they are waiting to hear arguments supporting what they already think.

Jurors bring their earlier impressions and judgments into closing argument. Their views may have evolved during the evidence, or they may have remained stubbornly attached to their initial feelings about the case. Some parts of the trial will be remembered better than others. This will hold true for each juror individually. Some may be skeptical. Others may be impatient. Most will likely be tired, uncomfortable from hours of sitting, and anxious to get back to their own lives.

Good lawyers have a sense of where the jurors are before they begin to close the case.

Jurors may want to hear about specific topics. For example, they may be looking for guidance on damages in a tort case, or specific elements in a criminal case. They may have questions about affirmative defenses. They may be wondering what the lawyers will say about a difficult witness, or how one side will deal with very strong evidence from the other side. Good lawyers anticipate these topics. They make sure the closing covers any questions hovering over the case.

What are these unspoken questions? Is there a way to answer these questions that will be persuasive? Frustrated jurors may drift toward the other side if the opposing lawyer is better at answering the unspoken questions.

Closing is a time to realize the full potential of favorable evidence without crossing over to exaggeration. It is also a time to reach as many jurors as possible. For example, assume a *likeable* or sympathetic witness for the opponent has made inconsistent statements. Is the witness mistaken? Does the witness have a bad memory? Is the witness trying to help a friend? Is the witness under pressure? Is the witness untruthful? At closing, a good lawyer will land somewhere in the zone of the first three options, because several jurors will likely come along. It is *less* likely jurors will move all the way to "untruthful":

We know the nephew, Jack Dunn, has said three different things about the accident. (Lawyer displays three different statements on the screen)

1) We were singing, and I didn't notice the traffic light.

2) The light turned yellow after we already passed the crosswalk.

3) The light was red for our side.

Members of the jury, you decide. Some of you may find that Mr. Dunn is in a very difficult place in this lawsuit. Some may find that he has a bad memory. Some may find that he is not truthful. Whatever the reason, he can't help us understand what happened. Any way you see it, we cannot *rely* on his testimony.

CLOSING ARGUMENT IS THE TIME TO TELL THE JURORS *HOW* TO DECIDE THE CASE AND *WHY* IT SHOULD BE DECIDED THAT WAY.

A good lawyer supports each argument with key facts. The themes of the case should resonate throughout the closing. The *why* part of closing may necessarily include an explanation of the law that applies to the case. If it is important to address the law in closing, it should be done in a juror- friendly way. Long-winded recitations of jury instructions are boring and distracting.

One of the subtle points of lawyering is to keep some distance from the emotional center of the case. Anger is not a persuasive trial tool. Sarcasm is not a persuasive trial tool. When lawyers are too angry or flippant, jurors pull away. Melodrama is insincere, and sincerity is critical for credibility. If a lawyer communicates (even unintentionally) to jurors that the evidence is not the important thing in the case, they will pull away. The goal is to be interesting and engaging, with a degree of emotion appropriate to the story.

Powerful facts speak for themselves. Rather than ranting, good lawyers remind jurors of the emotional power in the case through exhibits and testimony.

WHAT ARE THE BEST ARGUMENTS, AND WHAT FACTS SUPPORT EACH ARGUMENT?

Persuasive closings are organized. Arguments should be clear and succinct. They may be organized by issue, witness, party, fact groups, or burden. Compelling facts should be drawn in to support each argument. Closing is not a time to simply stand in front of the jury and recite the testimony again. It is the time to argue the merits. Lawyers are not court reporters. The goal is to persuade.

Closing is the time to emphasize the most helpful aspects of the case. Sometimes the sheer volume of helpful facts is worth a lot. Sometimes credibility arguments are more helpful. In other cases, the burden may be a better focus. Every helpful argument should be considered. More arguments mean more options for jurors when it comes time for them to hang their hats. Some will be moved by one argument, and others may be strongly influenced by an entirely different argument.

Language is important. A good lawyer is not ambivalent, apologetic, or vague in closing.

STAY INSIDE THE EVIDENCE AND THE LAW.

Closing arguments should be based on the facts and law of the case. Lawyers who attempt to appeal to jurors by "flag-waving", inciting fear, or making personal attacks on the opposing side are stepping outside the appropriate bounds of advocacy. Contemporaneous objections should be made by the injured side when this occurs. Improper arguments are also grounds for a mistrial.[25]

"Public policy" arguments are objectionable. For example, there is universal agreement that murder is bad, and that innocent people need to be protected. However, those arguments do nothing to prove whether a specific defendant *committed* a murder. Some people may think tort reform is a good idea, but that concept does nothing to prove whether an individual plaintiff has been wronged under existing laws.

At closing, lawyers should keep in mind that they are not in front of a legislative body, a city commission, or a community task force. Trials are not town hall meetings. [26]

---

25   *See* Boucher v. Glass, 874 So.2d 701 (Fla. App.1st Dist. 2004); Cole v. State, 866 So.2d 761(Fla. App. 1st Dist. 2004).

26   It is important to object when opposing counsel makes inflammatory arguments. A motion for mistrial should also be made.

Good lawyers give jurors guidance without delivering a lecture or getting bogged down in too much detail. It is *key* details that matter. If there are facts speaking loudly for the other side, a good lawyer addresses them in the best way possible. Are there strong competing facts? Is there a credibility issue which neutralizes the other side's facts? Is there a critical element which has been overlooked or downplayed by the other side?

Some lawyers ramble aimlessly during closing argument. They waste valuable time thanking jurors for their service, thanking jurors for listening, thanking jurors for their patience, apologizing for the length of the trial, explaining what closing argument *will* be, and so forth. This unfortunate practice signals to the jury that there aren't any good arguments to be made. As the jurors hear it, lawyers try to curry favor when they don't have anything else on their client's side. Lawyers with a strong case talk about the *case.*

It takes more effort to be professional, but it matters. A good lawyer demonstrates *true* respect and courtesy for the jury during the *entire* trial by being punctual, well-prepared, and professional. Closing argument should be helpful. Closing argument should be about the *case.*

In closing, each side should have an opportunity to present arguments *and* respond to the arguments of the other side. The party that initiated the lawsuit usually gets to present the first argument. This is usually the plaintiff or the prosecution. The defense should then be permitted to respond to the other side's argument and present the defense closing (they may overlap). The plaintiff/prosecution should then have an opportunity for rebuttal.

Rebuttal argument should be limited to topics covered by the opposing side. It is objectionable for the side with "the last word" to try and raise *new* points when the opponent has no further chance to respond.

SAMPLES OF CLOSING ARGUMENT.

Plaintiff in wrongful death/ medical negligence case:

Simple things can save lives. Simple care. Simple competence.
Members of the jury, there are two issues in this case. The first is whether the care and treatment provided to Mr. Lane by the defendants fell below the

standard of care for emergency medical providers in Jackson County in 2015. The answer is it did. The second issue is whether the defendants, by failing to monitor Mr. Lane's breathing tube, caused his death. The answer is yes, they did.

Let's start with the first issue. The defendants have admitted they failed to monitor Mr. Lane's breathing tube. There is no dispute about it. Once they got the tube properly inserted on the second attempt, and they had Mr. Lane on oxygen, they did not monitor the tube. On route to the hospital, they were not checking to see if the tube remained in place.

These tubes become dislodged—that is not the issue. The issue is whether the defendants *noticed* so they could either get it back in place or use one of the other available methods to make sure Mr. Lane was getting oxygen.

(Displaying list on screen) Here are three of the ways the defendants could have monitored Mr. Lane's breathing tube. These are simple ways they could have noticed and, if needed, started breathing for him again.

The first way is to check for moisture. If things were working right, moisture should have been present here (using exhibit). Or, they could have used this device, which can be attached to the tube (showing 2d exhibit). If things were working right, the color here would have changed from tan to purple and back to tan again. This shows us that oxygen and other gases are moving as they should be and oxygen is going where it should go. They could have used a stethoscope (3rd exhibit). Simple. None of these things happened.

Instead, oxygen which should have gone to Mr. Lane's lungs ended up in his stomach.

This failure, the failure to monitor the breathing tube, fell below the standard of care for emergency medicine in Jackson County in 2015. We know this from witnesses on both sides. Dr Cowart, a nationally known expert in anesthesiology and critical care medicine, explained the standard of care to us. The defendant's own expert agreed with this. This is another point that is not in dispute.

Let's move to the second issue. The defendant's failure to monitor the breathing tube caused the death of Michael Lane. That is why Michael's wife, Pricilla Lane, sits in this courtroom today as a widow.

How do we know this?

(displaying x-ray on the screen) The tube ended up here (pointing to the stomach area).

These tubes are challenging to insert. On the second attempt, the defendants were able to successfully place the tube here (pointing to the wind pipe). Mr. Lane was getting the oxygen he needed to survive. He had a pulse. He was moving.

Then the tube became dislodged. They were not checking, so they missed it. If they had checked, if they had monitored, they would have noticed. They could have attempted to reinsert the tube. Or, they could have started breathing for him again as they had before he was intubated. They could have put a mask back on him.

None of those things happened. Oxygen intended for Mr. Lane's lungs ended up in his stomach. His stomach was swollen with oxygen. Distended. Remember how the ER doctor described him. His diaphragm was compressed. He couldn't breathe. His brain was deprived of oxygen-- essential for life. This is what killed him.

Simply put, but for the defendant's failure, Mr. Lane would have survived.

The defendants have tried to convince you that Mr. Lane was already dying when they arrived at his house. We know this isn't true. Their own records show Mr. Lane's vital signs were getting stronger, not weaker. (displaying EMT notes on screen) When the defendants arrived, Mr. Lane had a pulse. He had survived that critical period of maximum saturation. The drug's effects had already peaked. He was *moving*. (referencing notes) When they gave him narcan, they had to use restraints. The oxycodone didn't kill him. The defendant's negligence killed him.

Find the defendants liable for the death of Michael Lane.

Defense in a burglary trial:

Members of the jury, the state hasn't even proven that this was a burglary, let alone an armed burglary. Even if we used our imagination and imagined they proved a burglary, they haven't proven Mr. Griffin is the person who was in Ms. Dante's house that night.

This whole case is about imagination. Every time we get to a critical place in the story, we need to use our imagination, because there is no proof. That works for fiction, but not for a real trial.

Ms. Dante didn't report a burglary until one of the neighbors told Ms. Dante's *husband* about a strange car parked in front of their house.

Let's look at some of the things Ms. Dante has said: She said she was asleep when the house was burglarized. She said she is a sound sleeper. That's odd, because we know she was sending text messages and posting to Facebook during the time she claims she was asleep (referring to exhibits on screen).

Ms. Dante also says the burglar took a handgun from a drawer in her bedroom, but she can't remember the make, the model, or even the color of the gun. She says it was a semi-automatic handgun, not a revolver. That's the only thing she seems to be sure of.

The only gun any of the witnesses have ever seen Mr. Griffin with is a revolver. If we want evidence that Mr. Griffin had a semi-automatic handgun, we will have to imagine it.

That's not good enough. The state has not proven a crime occurred. They have not proven Mr. Griffin is guilty of anything. Not proven. Find him not guilty.

Defense in a premises liability trial:

In a perfect world, accidents would not happen, and people would not get hurt. Members of the jury, ours is a wonderful world, but it is not a perfect one. Accidents do happen, and even when people are doing things right, someone can get hurt. The plaintiff got hurt in this case, but it was not because of anything Ms. Borden did, and it was not because of anything Ms. Borden failed to do.

Ms. Borden is not to blame for the plaintiff's injuries. The shoes, the wine, and the plaintiff's impatience are to blame.

(holding shoe) The plaintiff was wearing this type of shoe when she came into the restaurant with her party. (displaying picture from social media showing plaintiff at the restaurant). These shoes have 5-inch heels. These are the shoes she was wearing on the stairs. Remember the EMT's testimony.

Every witness from the party agreed on one thing— the public parking lot where they parked is a gravel lot. The plaintiff and her friends parked back here (displaying picture). They had to walk all the way through the lot and then 3 city blocks to get to Ms. Borden's restaurant. They asked for a table upstairs, because they had a large party and they wanted to be seated together.

The plaintiff complained about her shoes that night. She said they were hard to walk in, and she considered taking them off. She admitted this in her testimony. The shoes were hard to walk in, but she kept them on. We see them in the pictures. The EMT's had to take the shoes off.

The plaintiff and her friends were drinking wine that evening. They had a large bottle on the table, and glasses were being refilled as they were emptied. Here is the plaintiff (picture on screen) with her glass. The plaintiff was at the restaurant for more than an hour before she went back down the stairs. For an hour plus, she is at the table drinking and celebrating. Here is the alcohol tab (receipt on screen). That's for 5 people. That's 3 bottles of wine.

Why did she go down the left stairwell? She wanted her phone charger. She didn't want to wait. The front stairwell was *momentarily* off limits while a waiter cleaned up a spill. Was anything wrong with the left stairwell? No.

Members of the jury, no one else had a problem with the left stairwell in the restaurant that evening. The plaintiff has to *prove* an unsafe condition. The only witness who claimed the rubber strip on the third stair was loose wasn't *sure* about it, remember? The only employee who said the rubber strips were loose was the ex-employee, John Stovall. He was in a dispute with Ms. Borden over the house rules, remember?

Ms. Borden did not cause the plaintiff's injuries. Find Molly Borden and Borden's Garden Eatery not liable.

Civil rights case with unpopular speaker:

Members of the jury, truth is important. Justice is important. In jury selection, we talked about what your role would be if you were chosen to hear Mr. Shea's case. Ultimately, you will decide what justice is in this case. This trial is not a popularity contest. It isn't about being likeable, successful, or even friendly. The law is for everyone, as we discussed in jury selection. The law applies to everyone and the law is for the benefit of everyone. The same laws apply to popular people and unpopular people. We are asking each of you to remember this when you discuss Mr. Shea's case. You will be in the privacy and sanctity of the jury room. When you go in to decide this case, it will be about the proof, the facts, and not popularity. It will be about finding truth.

Defense in aggravated assault case:

Mr. Rollins admitted here in court that he had already closed the door before Cole threw the flower pot. Mr. Rollins wasn't in fear, he was angry. He didn't even know about the flower pot until he heard some racket at the door and went to see what it was. Cole isn't on trial for failing to be a model nephew. He isn't on trial for irritating his Uncle. He is on trial for aggravated assault. In a moment, the judge will tell you that one of the elements of aggravated assault is that the victim must be placed in *fear.*

Mr. Rollins wanted Cole out of the house. He never wanted to share the house with his nephew in the first place. He had no choice at the outset, because Cole's father was a co-owner. It never worked out. Anger clouds everything Mr. Rollins told you today.

Prosecutor in a murder trial:

This shooting was not in self-defense. It was for revenge. It was for spite. "It's coming back around"(referencing text on screen). This is what the defendant texted to the victim about 20 minutes before the shooting. What was coming back around? The defendant was very angry about *this* (putting state's exhibit, slide of SUV with custom rims, on the screen). The victim persuaded Mike Summer to sell this beautiful new SUV to him instead of the defendant. The defendant was enraged about this. He found out about it the day before the shooting. How do we know this? The Defendant was so angry that he threw a beer bottle through the window of his own apartment. He threatened the victim in front of three witnesses. One of these witnesses was a new neighbor who knows no one involved in this case and has absolutely no reason to make this stuff up.

These shots were fired outside the club, not inside the club. Remember the victim's girlfriend, Tabatha Miles, told you she had the victim's cellphone inside the club that night because she was waiting to find out when her Mom's flight got in. (picking up state's exhibit, the cell phone) Here is the cell phone, members of the jury, and it is bloody. We know from the analysts who testified this week that the blood on this phone is the victim's blood. The victim was bleeding before he got into the club. He was bleeding when he picked up this phone. He was running away.

PROFESSIONAL IDENTITY

PROFESSIONALISM IS AN IDENTITY, NOT JUST A WAY OF
ACTING.
PROFESSIONALISM EMBRACES AND SURROUNDS ETHICS.
PROFESSIONAL IDENTITY BEGINS IN LAW SCHOOL.
PROFESSIONALISM SHOULD BECOME SECOND NATURE.
NO LAWYER IS PERFECT, BUT SOME LAWYERS ARE BETTER
THAN OTHERS AT DEALING WITH THEIR OWN MISTAKES.

Professionalism is more than an aspiration. It is more than a goal, and it is broader than conduct or disciplinary rules. From the first day of law school, students should be mindful of the essential attributes of the legal profession. Will they enter a highly skilled profession defined by honor, trust, and service, or will they simply look for a job that requires a law degree? Will they meet the challenges and demands of lawyering with patience and courage, or will they adopt made-for-television work habits? Will they think mostly in terms of monthly bank statements, or will they develop a long-range plan that is more reflective?

Lawyers are highly visible and therefore most subject to scrutiny when they are in the courtroom. Trials are public. Trial lawyers play a key role in the public perception of the legal profession. The pressure to *prevail* in trial is great. The desire to "look good" in front of jurors and clients is part of being human. Some lawyers are tempted to treat professionalism as a mode that they can control with an "on-and-off" switch.

The reality is that professionalism is not something to be picked up when convenient and cast off again for expediency. Lawyers who try to maintain a professional façade in the courtroom are not likely to succeed. True professionalism becomes second nature. It is consistent and constant, regardless of changes or difficulties in cases, opponents, schedules, personal circumstances, or fortunes. It is reflective as opposed to reactive.

Young lawyers should ask themselves this question: Do I want to be defined by a case, a verdict, an argument, an income bracket? Or, do I want to be defined by who I *am*?

Lawyers are ultimately measured by the value they ascribe to professionalism. Win/loss records and dollar judgments are based on the types of cases lawyers handle and the facts of those cases. These have little relation to the professional identity of the lawyer. Popularity is not professionalism. Bragging rights do not attach to professionalism. Professionalism includes thought, conduct, and self-image. It is an *identity*. The rewards that flow from a professional law practice are broader, more complex, and more permanent than material wealth.

A mistake is made when lawyers equate professionalism with ethics. Ethical rules are the law for lawyers. A code of ethics for law practice is in place in some form in every jurisdiction. There is usually a bright line test and a clearly defined course of action under a code of ethics. Professionalism necessarily embraces ethics, but it extends far beyond.

From the time they enter law school, aspiring lawyers should think about how they will structure their practice and the way law practice will fit into their lives. How important is it to be a member of the legal profession? How much influence do individual lawyers have on the public perception of justice? Does it matter? Is it possible to find a happy and well-balanced life between the courtroom and the home? Will it be rewarding to practice law? How much will reputation matter?

Lawyers are called upon to make decisions and exercise judgment every day in every aspect of practice. Law is a service profession with high stakes for clients. The highest standards of professionalism should dictate everything from the way office interviews are conducted to the way a cross examination or closing argument is handled.

No lawyer should practice in an isolated environment, because isolation leads to stress. Even sole practitioners should avail themselves of professional resources. Resources are important at every level and every stage of practice. Resources include colleagues, support staff, bar organizations, legal data bases, and professional services. Experience is also a resource. The value of lessons learned is great. Lawyers need to develop inner resources to cope with the normal stress and demands of practice.

In stressful situations, it is a good idea to pause, take a deep breath, and *think* before speaking. A good lawyer puts some distance between the immediate, emotional reaction and an actual response to judges, other lawyers, e-mails, texts, or phone messages.

All lawyers make mistakes. To the extent humanly possible, *big* mistakes should be avoided. Within ethical boundaries, a lawyer must first be a loyal and prepared advocate for a client. The next consideration should be courteous and even generous treatment of colleagues, opposing lawyers, employees, court personnel, and anyone else within the orbit of the lawyer's practice.

In day-to-day life, lawyers send a message to all those around them about their professional identity. The message gets out, whether intended or not. Lawyers earn reputations—some good, some bad.

LAWYERS SHOULD.

Dress in comfortable, well-fitting business clothes. A basic guideline for jewelry, make-up, or hair is that it should not be distracting.

Have copies of case law, jury instructions, and motions for opposing counsel and the judge.

Get enough sleep while preparing for trial and trying the case.

Allow time for scheduled and spontaneous recreation/relaxation breaks during preparation.

Review the entire case and all strategy decisions or concerns with co-counsel before the trial.

Go over the trial process and the client's role with the client as early as possible during trial preparation.

Have a pretrial conference with opposing counsel (this is mandatory in many jurisdictions). All discovery rules should be followed. Stipulations or agreements which can be entered without detriment to the client should be considered.

Make sure everyone on the trial team knows which lawyer has responsibility for each part of the trial.

Check notes periodically during the trial to make sure everything is covered on behalf of the client.

Make the court aware of any stipulations entered with opposing counsel.

Make a note pad and pen available during trial so the client can jot down notes or communicate without causing disruption.

Address the judge, the clerks, and the bailiffs with courtesy.

Take deep breaths, maintain a gracious temperament, and handle bad rulings or a bad verdict with grace.

Make an early and sincere apology to colleagues or opposing counsel when a stressful day or a particularly difficult case has caused friction, ill temper, or hostility.

LAWYERS SHOULD NOT.

Wear distracting clothes or jewelry. It isn't about the lawyers. It's about the case and the client.

Make editorial comments or remarks in jury range, no matter how annoying the other party is. Sidebars and bench conferences are intended to be outside of juror earshot for important reasons.

Thank the judge for rulings. Rulings are not favors, they are legal decisions.

Leave easels or exhibits in front of jurors when the other party is conducting examinations (unless both sides are using the exhibit with the witness).

Talk audibly at counsel table while other lawyers or witnesses are speaking, except as necessary to make objections.

Roll the eyes, glare, laugh, cough loudly, rattle papers, or engage in other distracting behavior while other lawyers are conducting parts of the trial.

Stay up all night before the trial.

Make personal attacks on opposing counsel.

Hold grudges, or make *any* trial decision based on a desire for revenge or animosity toward an opposing lawyer. The client's interests are what matters.

Talk about themselves, their own family members, their law practices, their personal opinions, or their personal views about the case in the presence of jurors.

Give personal testimonials for their clients, their witnesses, or the credibility of the evidence during the trial.

TWO UNDERRATED ADVANTAGES FOR TRIAL LAWYERS ARE EMOTIONAL AND PHYSICAL WELLNESS.

The demands of trial practice are less stressful and more rewarding for lawyers who care for themselves. It is not vanity or conceit that make the career better. It is genuine attention to life balance and physical wellbeing. Lawyers who are seriously motivated to do a good job for their clients include sleep, nutritional food, and regular exercise in their daily lives. They have hobbies and other non-law interests. In their busy schedules, they factor in time to do absolutely nothing. They get away, mentally and physically, from the office. It is easier to focus on work when other parts of life get meaningful attention as well.

PREPARE IN ADVANCE FOR A POSSIBLE "EMERGENCY."

Law students should discuss possible ways to resolve highly stressful trial situations while they are in the relative comfort and safety of the school environment. Good lawyers also do this in the safety of their offices, before they walk into court. It is part of mental preparation. All lawyers have "crisis" days in practice, but trial lawyers are uniquely vulnerable. Trials are adversarial proceedings. If other methods of dispute resolution have failed, it is likely the litigants have a lot at stake. Clients bring their own anxiety and stress to the trial. There are many variables in trial practice. There are judges, jurors, and numerous witnesses. There are many different personalities. Every person in the case has an ego, an agenda, and a boiling point.

Naturally, lawyers want to feel as if they are in complete control of their cases. In a strict sense, this is never possible.

Nerves can wear thin. Frustration can boil over during discovery, informal meetings, pretrial hearings, conferences, phone calls, e-mails, and trial.

For these reasons, it is wise to have a variety of possible options in mind for emergency moments. Emergency moments are those that may damage a lawyer's professional identity, a client's chances, or both. Depending on the situation, possible emergency responses include:

(If the jury is present) Asking for a recess.
Asking for a moment to confer with co-counsel.
Walking away.

Attempting to calm an angry opponent (taking the high road).

Taking some deep breaths.

Taking a deep breath and saying/typing/texting nothing.

Taking the rest of the morning/afternoon off.

Calling a good friend or loved one and listening to a supportive, friendly voice.

(Always) Remembering that this unpleasant experience will soon be a day, a week, a month, a year, and ultimately many years *ago*.

Don't let it matter too much.

Don't give it too much value.

FAMOUSLY DANGEROUS MYTHS AND HALF-TRUTHS OF TRIAL ADVOCACY

Myth 1: The jurors decide the case in jury selection.

Myth 2: Be argumentative in opening statement if you can get away with it.

Myth 3: Cover the bad facts during direct exam so you can defeat the cross exam.

Myth 4: Object just to throw the other side off.

Myth 5: It's the question that is important in cross exam-- the answer doesn't matter.

Myth 6: Don't object during closing argument. It's rude.

Like most myths, the often-heard tales of trial advocacy contain bits of truth. Some of them are even helpful in certain cases. However, the truthful bits are lost in the wholesale adoption of generalizations. Well-meaning but bad advice is often passed down from generation to generation of young lawyers.

It is important to debunk these myths. They are poor substitutes for good judgment and common sense. They are also at odds with the true goals in each part of a trial. A few of the most common and dangerous myths and half-truths of trial advocacy are addressed here.

MYTH 1: THE JURORS MAKE UP THEIR MINDS IN JURY SELECTION.

Don't assume the jurors will decide the case in jury selection. If the selection process is fair and lawyers for each side use good judgment and skill in the exercise of strikes, remaining jurors should be waiting anxiously to hear the case. They should be anxious to *learn* the facts and withhold judgment until they know everything and hear arguments from both sides.

It's a popular myth that cases are decided in jury selection. The truth about jury selection is less dramatic but nonetheless important. First impressions are strong and lasting. Lawyers who conduct jury selection with a positive attitude and a respectful but straightforward approach to their questions usually leave jurors with an idea that the case is strong for their clients.

MYTH 2: ARGUE AS MUCH AS POSSIBLE IN OPENING.

In opening statements, it is important to capture the respect and attention of each juror. Lawyers who are overly argumentative in opening are taking a risk. They are gambling that jurors will be more inclined toward the side that is already in battle mode. They are assuming it is persuasive to be combative at the outset of the trial.

Jurors may become frustrated or even angry with lawyers who are essentially arguing the case in a vacuum. At opening, jurors have not heard the witnesses or seen any evidence. They want to know what happened and why it matters. They don't want to feel pressured into a position without an opportunity to hear the case. Lawyers who do positive, fact-rich openings are likely to be more successful than lawyers who argue the merits in a case the jurors have not yet heard.

It is helpful for jurors to hear facts. Helpful lawyers have an edge, because the jurors sense they have a case that will stand on its own feet. Like many aspects of advocacy and persuasion, it's a matter of degree.

Argumentative openings are objectionable. It is hardly persuasive to begin a trial faced with repeated sustained objections due to overly contentious remarks. It is also tedious and repetitive to continually preface opening remarks with, "The evidence will show..." This overused phrase does not make an argumentative opening any less so.

It is natural to want to give a client as much advantage as possible during opening statements. This can be done effectively by making the jurors aware of key issues in the case and alerting them to critical aspects of evidence that may ultimately make or break the case. Good lawyers *explain why* certain evidence will be very important. They use contrasts, and they emphasize facts that will be difficult or impossible for the opposing side to overcome. This is the bit of truth in the myth.

If the opening is positive and fact-rich, lawyers can comfortably incorporate important themes. They can alert jurors to the controversies which brought the parties to court in the first place. They can leave the jurors with a keen interest in listening to the evidence. In a good opening, jurors will know what to expect in the evidence, and why it matters.

MYTH 3: GET ALL THE BAD FACTS OUT ON DIRECT TO TAKE THE WIND OUT OF THE OPPONENT'S CROSS EXAM.

This is a dangerous myth. It is especially dangerous for parties with the burden of proof. Lawyers who put too many bad facts in a direct examination end up sending a mixed message to jurors. Is this a good witness or not? Is this credible evidence or not? The overall effect of including too much baggage on direct is to end up with an ambivalent jury.

The truth requires more thought. There are certain types of information that should be addressed up front by the side calling a witness. The decision whether to include bad facts during direct should be based on credibility. For example, prosecutors should let jurors know about plea agreements with their key witnesses. Parties who must call a witness with *major* inconsistent statements should address the prior statements during direct and have the witness explain them if possible.

Less damaging inconsistencies or biases should be handled on a wait-and-see basis. Where possible, the witness should be prepared for cross. If necessary, some rehabilitation can be done with redirect examination. Sometimes the best way to handle bad facts is to be dismissive or ignore them altogether. It depends. It is not a one-size-fits-all.

Binging out bad facts is rarely going to prevent the cross examiner from gaining mileage in the same area. Adverse parties have a right to confront and cross examine witnesses. Lawyers who buy into this myth end up calling more attention to bad facts by getting them in front of the jury too early and too often.

MYTH 4: MAKE OBJECTIONS JUST TO THROW THE OTHER SIDE OFF.

Jurors are frustrated by objections. Objections interrupt the story. Lawyers who repeatedly object are sort of like movie-goers who keep walking in front of the screen on their way to the refreshment counter. It is especially annoying when they interrupt the action at exciting points.

Frivolous objections only highlight harmful evidence. They are usually over-ruled. Jurors notice when a lawyer makes repeated "losing" objections. The truth is that harmful evidence should be dealt with in a more sophisticated and thoughtful way. Is there a way to neutralize or counter the harmful evidence? Can it be addressed in a helpful way during cross examination, or through another witness?

Jurors also notice facial expressions and body language of lawyers and clients. When the opponent is getting harmful facts from a witness, it is important to keep a "poker face."

Objections should only be made when 1) there is a valid legal basis for an objection, and 2) the evidence or argument is harmful to the client.

MYTH 5: THE QUESTION IS THE IMPORTANT THING IN CROSS EXAM. IT DOESN'T MATTER HOW THE WITNESS ANSWERS.

Answers matter during cross examination. If the point is needed for closing, it must be admitted or established somewhere else in the evidence. *Asking* alone is not enough to establish evidence for purposes of argument.

Another concern is the jury, and what jurors are apt to do with denials from witnesses. Lawyers should be realistic about cross exam. They should not assume jurors will adopt the premise behind a question when the witness (especially a likeable witness) has denied it. Jurors will watch the witness and make observations about the way the question is handled. If the witness is strong, the wildcard question may be a disaster.

This myth is an unrealistic extension of an important truth. On cross, lawyers should ask leading questions (statements of fact) calculated to take away from the other side and add to the cross-examiner's side. The question should be a statement, and the statement should be deadly. The answer is still important.

MYTH 6: IT IS RUDE TO OBJECT DURING CLOSING ARGUMENTS.

Notwithstanding the growing number of reversals for improper closing argument, this myth is still alive. Lawyers have an obligation to protect their clients from unfair argument and improper conduct.

Objections can and should be made in a professional manner. They should only be made when there is a valid legal basis to do so. Lawyers who fail to make valid objections to harmful, improper arguments fail their obligations to their clients. It is not rude to protect a client from unfair arguments. It is a professional obligation to do so.

XI. Appendix

CROSS EXAMINATION (SCOPE AND IMPEACHMENT).

Calhoun v. Florida, 502 So. 2d 1364 (Fla. App. 2nd Dist. 1987)

Freeman v. Florida, 846 So. 2d 552 (Fla. App.4th Dist. 2003)

Michael v. Florida, 884 So. 2d 83 (Fla. App.2nd Dist. 2004)

Foster v. Florida, 869 So. 2d 743 (Fla .App.2nd Dist. 2004)

Hunter v. Maryland, 397 Md. 580(Ct. App. Md. 2007)

Jackson v. Florida, 881 So. 2d 711 (Fla. App.3rd Dist. 2004)

James v. Florida, 765 So. 2d 763 (Fla. App. 1st Dist. 2000)

Howard v. Florida, 869 So. 2d 725 (Fla. App.2nd Dist. 2004)

Lomax v. Mississippi, 192 So.3d 975 (Sup.Ct. Miss. 2016)

Parfenuk v. Georgia, 789 S.E.2d 332 (Ct. App. Ga. 2016)

California v. Sanchez, 63 Cal. 4th 665 (Sup. Ct. Cal.2016)

Colorado v. Dunham, 381 P.3d 415 (Co. Ct .App. 2016)

Illinois v. McCoy, Ill. App. (1st) 130988 (2016)

Illinois v. Gaston, 147 A.D. 3d 1219 (Sup. Ct. App. Div. 3d Dept. N.Y. 2017)

Smith v. Georgia, 796 S.E.2d (Sup. Ct. Ga. 2017)

Vantran Industries, Inc. v. Ryder Truck Rental, Inc., 890 So. 2d 421 (Fla. App.1st Dist. 2004)

U.S. v. Grant, 256 F. 3d 1146 (11th Cir. 2001)

EXPERT WITNESS TESTIMONY.

Gutierrez v. Vargas, 239 So.3d 615 (Fla. 2018) WL 1417553

Lamb v. State, --- So. 3d --- (Fla. App 4th Dist. 2018) WL 2049640

Sanchez v. Cinque, 238 So. 3d 817 (Fla. App. 4th Dist. 2018)

Daubert v. Merrell Dow Pharmaceuticals, 509 U.S. 579 (1993)

Boudreaux v. Bollinger Shipyard, 197 So. 3d 761 (La. App. 4th Cir. 2016)

Worley v. Central Florida YMCA, 228 So. 3d 18 (Fla. 2018)

Andrews v. State, 181 So. 3d 526 (Fla. App. 5th Dist. 2015)

Castillo v. Dupont De Nemours & Co., 854 So. 2d 1264 (Fla. 2000)

Cordoba and Gibbs v. Rodriguez, 939 So.2d 319 (Fla. App. 4th Dist. 2006)

Florida v. Demeniuk, 888 So. 2d 655 (Fla. App.5th Dist. 2004)

Florida v. Sercey, 825 So.2d 959 (Fla. App. 1st Dist. 2002)

Fragogiannis v. Sisters of St. Francis, Ill. App. (1st) 141788(2015)

Halcomb v. Washington Metropolitan Transit, 526 F. Supp. 2d 24 (U.S.D.C. Dist. Col. 2007)

Mackerly v. Florida, 900 So.2d 662 (Fla. App. 4th Dist. 2005)

Maryland v. Payne, 104 A.3d 142 (Ct. App. Md. 2014)

McClain v. Metabolife Intern Inc., 401 F. 3d 1233 (11th Cir. 2005)

New Jersey v. Spencer, 319 N.J. Super. 284 (Sup. Ct. N.J. 1999)

Padgett v. Sims, 701 So. 2d 357 (Fla. App. 1st Dist. 1997)

Ellingwood v. Stevens, 564 So. 2d 932 (Sup. Ct. Ala. 1990)

California v. Sanchez, 63 Cal. 4th 665 (Sup. Ct. Cal. 2016)

Briggs v. South Carolina, 806 S.E. 2d 713 (Sup. Ct. S.C. 2017)

IMPROPER LAY WITNESS OPINION/ INVADING PROVINCE OF THE JURY.

Bartlet v. Florida, 993 So. 2d 157 (Fla. App. 1st Dist. 2008)

Kolp v. Florida, 932 So. 2d 1283 (Fla. App. 4th Dist. 2006)

Griffin v. Florida, 872 So. 2d 998 (Fla. App 4th Dist. 2004)

Briggs v. South Carolina, 806 S.E. 2d 713 (Sup. Ct. S.C. 2017)

Lamb v. Florida, --- So. 3d --- (Fla. App 4th Dist. 2018)

HEARSAY AND EXCEPTIONS/NON-TRUTH USES.

Belvin v. Florida, 986 So.2d 516 (Sup. Ct. Fla. 2008)

Crawford v. Washington, 541 U.S. 36 (March 2004)

Briscoe v. Celebrity Cruises, Inc., 894 So.2d 294 (Fla. App. 3rd Dist. 2005)

Florence v. Florida, 905 So.2d 989 (Fla. App. 4th Dist. 2005)

Oregon v. Smith, 96 P. 3d 1234 (Ct. App. Ore. 2004)

U.S. v. Parry, 649 F. 2d 292 (5th Cir. 1981)

U.S. v. Bellinger, 652 Fed Appx 143 (4th Cir. 2016)

IMPROPER ARGUMENTS/ IMPROPER TRIAL CONDUCT.

Adams v. Florida, 830 So.2d 911 (Fla. App.3rd Dist. 2002)

Anderson v. Maryland, 135 A.3d 537 (Ct. Sp. App. Md. 2016)

Arizona v. Woodward, 516 P.2d 589 (Ct. App. Ariz.1973)

Bocher & McMurray v. Glass & Glass, 874 So. 2d 701 (Fla. App.1st Dist. 2004)

Cole v. Florida, 866 So.2d 761 (Fla. App.1st Dist. 2004)

Massachusetts v. Caruso, 476 Mass. 275 (Sup. Ct. Mass. 2017)

Pool v. Sup. Ct./State if Arizona, 139 Ariz. 98 (Sup. Ct. Ariz. *In banc*, 1984)

Robbins v. Florida, 891 So.2d 1102 (Fla. App. 5th Dist. 2005)

Georgia v. Orr, 812 S.E. 2d 137 (Ct. App. Ga. 2018)

New Jersey v. Smith, 770 A. 2d 255 (Sup. Ct. N.J. 2001)

North Carolina v. Dalton, 369 N.C. 311 (Sup. Ct. N.C. 2016)

Walker v. Maryland, 818 A.2d 1078 (Ct. App. Md. 2003)

Williams v. Florida, 877 So.2d 884 (Fla. App. 4th Dist. 2004)

JURY INSTRUCTIONS.

Barkett v. Gomez, 908 So. 2d 1084 (Fla. App. 3rd Dist.2005)

Briscoe v. Celebrity Cruises, Inc., 894 So. 2d 294 (Fla. App. 3rd Dist. 2005)

Corpstein v. Florida, 872 So. 2d 307 (Fla. App. 2nd Dist. 2004)

Dumas v. Florida, 907 So. 2d 560 (Fla. App. 4th Dist. 2005)

Van Loan v. Florida, 872 So. 2d 330 (Fla. App.2nd Dist. 2004)

Publix Super Markets v. Young, 848 So. 2d 1242 (Fla. App. 4th Dist. 2003) (verdict forms)

JURY SELECTION.

Busby v. Florida, 894 So. 2d 88 So. 2d (Fla. 2004)

Dorsey v. Florida, 868 So. 2d 1192 (Fla. 2003)

Payne v. Florida, 851 So. 2d 227 (Fla. App.4th Dist. 2003)

Boucher and McMurray v. Glass and Glass, 874 So. 2d 701 (Fla. App.1st Dist. 2004)

Howard v. Florida, 869 So. 2d 725 (Fla. App. 2nd Dist. 2004)

Jackson v. Florida, 881 So. 2d 711 (Fla. App. 3rd Dist. 2004)

Smith v. Florida, 253 So. 2d 465 (Fla. App.1st Dist. 1971)

Jaffe v. Applebaum, 830 So. 2d 136 (Fla. App.4th Dist. 2002)

Dardar v. Southern Distributors of Tampa, 563 So. 2d 1112 (Fla.1990)

Batson v. Kentucky, 476 U.S. 79 (1986) (race or gender-based strikes)

Oregon v. Ross, 961 P. 2d 241 (Ct. App. Ore. 1998)

Pennsylvania v. Edwards, 177 A. 3d 963 (Super. Ct. Pa. 2018)

Pennsylvania v. Garrett, 689 A. 2d 912 (Super. Ct. Pa. 1997)

Colorado v. Rodriguez, 351 P.3d 423 (Sup. Ct. Co. 2015)

MOTIONS FOR JUDGEMENT OF ACQUITTAL (CRIMINAL CASES).

E.S. v. Florida, 886 So. 2d 311 (Fla. App. 3rd Dist. 2004)

Garcia v. Florida, 899 So. 2d 447 (Fla. App. 4th Dist. 2005)

Walker v. Florida, 933 So. 2d 1236 (Fla. App. 3rd Dist. 2006)

MOTIONS FOR DIRECTED VERDICT (CIVIL CASES).

Kind and Kind v. Gittman, 889 So. 2d 87 (Fla. App.4th Dist. 2004)

PRESERVATION OF ERROR.

North Carolina v. Gullette, 796 S.E. 2d 396 (Ct. App. N.C. 2017)

Williams v. Florida 933 So. 2d 1254 (Fla. App. 1st Dist. 2006)

PRIVILEGE.

Lenz v. Florida, 183 So. 3d 1239 (Fla. App. 4th Dist. 2016)

Barkett v. Gomez, 908 So. 2d 1084 (Fla. App. 3rd Dist. 2005)

Bush v. Florida, 543 So. 2d 283 (Fla. App.2nd Dist. 1989)

Dodd v. Florida,537 So. 2d 626 (Fla. App.3rd Dist. 1988)

Jackson v. Florida, 738 So. 2d 382 (Fla. App.4th Dist. 1999)

England v. Florida, 940 So. 2d 389 (Fla. 2006) (photos)

Price v. Indiana, 765 N.E. 2d 1245 (Sup. Ct. Ind. 2002)

RULE OF COMPLETENESS.

Whitfield v. Florida, 933 So. 2d 1245 (Fla. App. 1st Dist. 2006)

SAMPLE FOUNDATIONS.

1. PHYSICAL ITEM — RED RUBBER BALL.

(Item previously marked with a letter for identification purposes, and eyewitness previously testified to seeing red ball crash through window of house)

Show the item to opposing counsel prior to asking the judge for permission to approach the witness.

Officer Rums, I'm showing you what's been marked for identification purposes as Plaintiff's exhibit 'A'. Please look at exhibit A and tell us whether you recognize it.

(Yes, I recognize this)

What is Plaintiff's exhibit A?

(This is the red rubber ball I collected inside the living room of the Tott's residence on the 15th of May)

How do you know recognize exhibit A as the ball you collected?

(It's the same shape, size, and color. Also, I placed my initials, the date, and the report number on one side on a piece of evidence tape)

Officer Rums, can you tell us whether Plaintiff's exhibit A is in substantially the same condition as it was on May 15th?
(Yes, it is)

Your Honor, we offer Plaintiff's exhibit A into evidence as Plaintiff's exhibit one.
(Admitted without objection)

May we show exhibit one to the jury?

2. PHOTOGRAPHIC IMAGE, DIAGRAM.

Preliminary steps are the same as above. The item has been pre-marked by letter, the witness has testified that a rubber ball came crashing into her house through her front bay window. The item has been shown to opposing counsel prior to asking permission to approach the witness.

Ms. Wynn, I'm showing you what's been pre-marked as Plaintiff's exhibit B for identification purposes. Would you please look at Plaintiff's B and tell us whether you recognize it?
(Yes– this is a picture of my house)

How do you recognize exhibit B?
(This is the front of the house, showing the window after the ball crashed through)

Ms. Wynn, is Plaintiff's exhibit B an accurate depiction of the front of your home on the afternoon of May 15th?
(Yes)

offer into evidence as Plaintiff's Two, ask permission to publish the photograph to the jurors.

3. BUSINESS RECORD.

Preliminary steps are the same as above. The witness provides general background and employment information. Next, the witness is asked:

Mr. Skat, how long have you worked at Community Medical Practice?
>(Three years.)

What are your duties for the Medical Practice?
>(I started out as an office assistant, and one year ago I was promoted to file manager. I maintain all of our patient files.)

In general, please describe your job responsibilities as they relate to patient files.
>(I pull files for the doctors and nurses when the patients come in, and at the conclusion of a patient visit, I obtain the file, check to make sure everything is in order, add notes from the current visit, and re-file the patient's information.)

When would a patient file be made or generated?
>(For any patient, any person seeking medical diagnosis or treatment from our physicians or nurse practitioners)

How often are the files updated?
>(Whenever a patient visits, or whenever there is any activity in the case– a new prescription, discontinuing a medication, and so on. The files are kept current as to each visit.)

Who provides the information that is kept in these files?
>(Doctors, nurses, patients, lab techs.)

How are patient files kept or maintained at Community Medical Practice?
>(We have both computer and hard copy files, and we maintain those in our file department at the office. We maintain records of all patient visits and all medical work done by our physicians.)

How long are these records kept or maintained?

(The Medical Group opened the practice seven and a half years ago, and we have records of all patient care from the first day onward)

For what purposes are these files maintained?

(For any legitimate purpose relating to the patient's care, patient treatment, and of course because doctors are professionally responsible for maintaining records of all medical care)

Mr. Skat, I'm showing you what's been previously marked as defense composite exhibit 'C' for identification purposes. Will you look at exhibit C and tell me whether you recognize it?

(Yes. This are the medical records of one of our patients at Community Medical Group.)

How do you recognize exhibit C as the record of one of your patients?

(I opened this file in 2017. I copied these records at the request of the patient and his attorney.)

Where have these records been kept since the file was opened in 2017?

(In our records department at the office.)

Where did the information contained in these records come from?

(From the treating physician, duty nurse, or medical assistants involved with patient care.)

When were these records made?

(At or immediately after the patient visits.)

Are the records in composite exhibit C those that are made and kept as a regular practice at Community Medical Group?

(Yes)

Your Honor, we offer defense composite exhibit C as defense exhibit four.

ACKNOWLEDGMENTS

Trying cases and teaching others how to try cases are happily communal efforts.

The author thanks her wonderful friends, colleagues, and mentors for their wisdom, courage, brilliance, friendship, humor, generosity, and honesty. A few of those wonderful people are Bill Miller, Bennett Hutson, Tania Alavi, Tom Farkash, Nick Zissimopolus, Karin Moore, Trisha Jenkins, Johnny Kearns, Susan Wehlburg, Carla Franklin, Bill Hoppe, Jeanne Singer, Rick Parker, Amy Mashburn, John Kelly, Terry Lenamon, Larry Turner, George Schaefer, Paul Zacks, Claire Luten, Scott Fingerhut, Kris Eisenmenger, Aaron Kelley, Stacy Scott, Linda Curry, Bob Dekle, Andy Slater, Judge Paul Huck, Judge Stephan Mickle, Judge James Colaw, Judge Peter Sieg, Judge Jenifer Harris, Judge Elzie Sanders, Judge Phyllis Kotey, Jennifer White, Carl Schwait, Craig DeThomasis, Rod Smith, Judge Jim Nilon, Judge Bill Davis, Alan Cohn, Susan Hugentugler, Caliene Lantz, Judge Joel Lazarus, Scott Richardson, Canaan Goldman, Brian Kramer, Neil Chonin, Judge Manny Menendez, Judge Samantha Ward, Judge Lisa Porter, Judge Denise Ferrero, Mac Heavener, Chuck Morton, Harvey Sepler, Judge Richard Hersch, Stuart Cohn, Jim Pierce, Fletcher Baldwin, Nancy Baldwin, Carl McGinnes, Ann Finnell, Jack Fine, Cherie Fine, Chuck Chance, Dr. Robert Kirby, Dr. Tonia Werner, Dr. Brian Cooke, Dr. Almari Ginory, Dr. Gary Reisfield, Dr. Matt Nguyen, Dan Vazquez, Darby Hertz, Elizabeth Waratuke, her late and dearly missed friends Margaret Stack and John Fischer, and the many wonderful, inspiring students she has been fortunate enough to have in her orbit over the years.